C000193120

TRANSIT BEIRUT
NEW WRITING AND IMAGES
Editors Malu Halasa and Roseanne Saad Khalaf

 SAQI   26 Westbourne Grove · London W2 5RH · www.saqibooks.com

Editors
Malu Halasa and Roseanne Saad Khalaf

Design
www.byboth.com

Translators
Marilyn Booth, Robin Bray, Sarah al-Hamad, David Macey

Copy-editing
Mitchell Albert, Yasmine Gaspard, Nupu Press

Contributors
Antoine Boulad, Rachid El Daif, Hasan Daoud, Zeina B. Ghandour, Ziad Halwani, Nabeel Kaakoush,
Kamal Kassar, Maher Kassar, Leila M., Reine Mahfouz, Lena Merhej, Omar Sabbagh, Hazim Saghie,
Nadine R.L. Touma, Fadi Tufayli, Abbas El-Zein

Photographers
Nabil Ismail and Dalia Khamissy

Cover photo: Paving the way for the reconstruction of downtown Beirut by Nabil Ismail, 1990

Thanks to Soukna El-Sayed Ali, Zeina Arida Bassil, Andy Cox, Dina Halawi Dally, I.F. Khoury at AUB,
Gabriel Khoury, Motassem Zahra and Mohamad Jaber at MAPS Geosystems (Beirut), Mai Ghoussoub,
Rasha Salti, Jacqui Stuart, Mark Glassner and Christine Tohme

British Library Cataloguing-in-Publication Data
A catalogue record for this book is available from the British Library

ISBN 0 86356 568 9

This edition first published 2004

Saqi Books
26 Westbourne Grove
London W2 5RH
www.saqibooks.com

INTRODUCTION

Malu Halasa and Roseanne Saad Khalaf

Beirut, a *mêlée* of pop culture chafing at tradition, occupies a special location in the mental geography of the Middle East. Its war-torn past and subsequent regeneration make it unique among contemporary Arab cities. The legacy of violence, and the resilience it created, are powerful factors in the search for a new identity.

For reasons of language, politics and economics, Arab fiction, memoir and photography are generally not widely available in the west. New writers suffer most of all. *Transit Beirut* is the first time that established writers such as Rachid El Daif, Hasan Daoud and Hazim Saghie are published together with fresh voices like Zeina B Ghandour, Nadine R.L. Touma, Lena Merhej and Omar Sabbagh. Some stories were specifically written for the anthology, others are newly translated from Arabic and French into English. All of them, to some extent, deal with individuals coming to terms with post-war Lebanon – sometimes in unexpected ways like food, music or avoiding plastic surgery.

Even at its most frenetic, shades of darkness lurk in *Transit Beirut*. A romantic rendezvous in an empty apartment becomes a lone vigil with a Kalashnikov. The bleak days of the 1982 Israeli invasion pose an unexpected philosophical question. The city's mid-1990s switch from war to commerce is documented through the voracious appetites of its inhabitants, whether for talking and eating 'American' or shopping in the latest suburban superstore. Reconstruction sculpted only part of the city's new face, leaving behind traces of an unsettled history.

To reduce the wide-ranging stories and visual essays in *Transit Beirut* to a single unifying viewpoint would be misleading. Yet all of them have been created by people who are formed by their affiliation to Beirut and its diverse culture. Clearly, it is these fears and aspirations that drive the city forward.

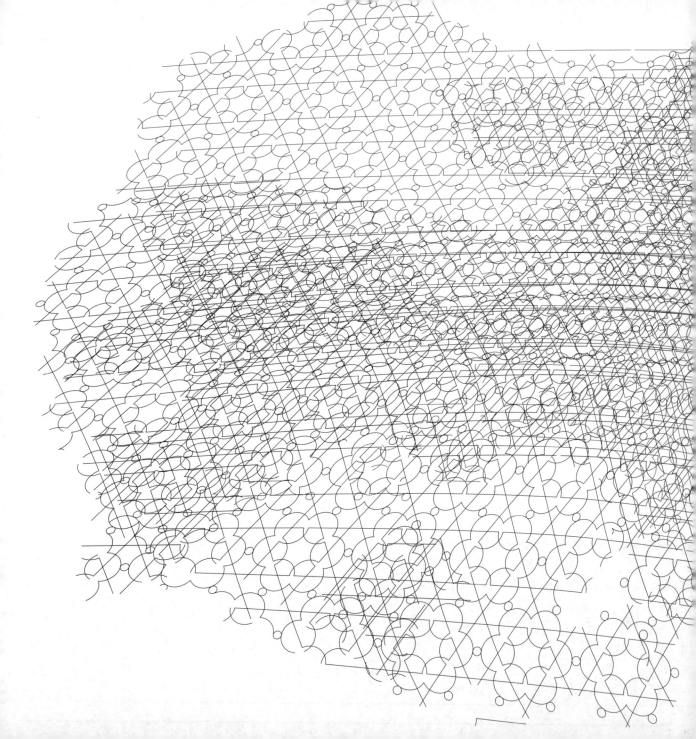

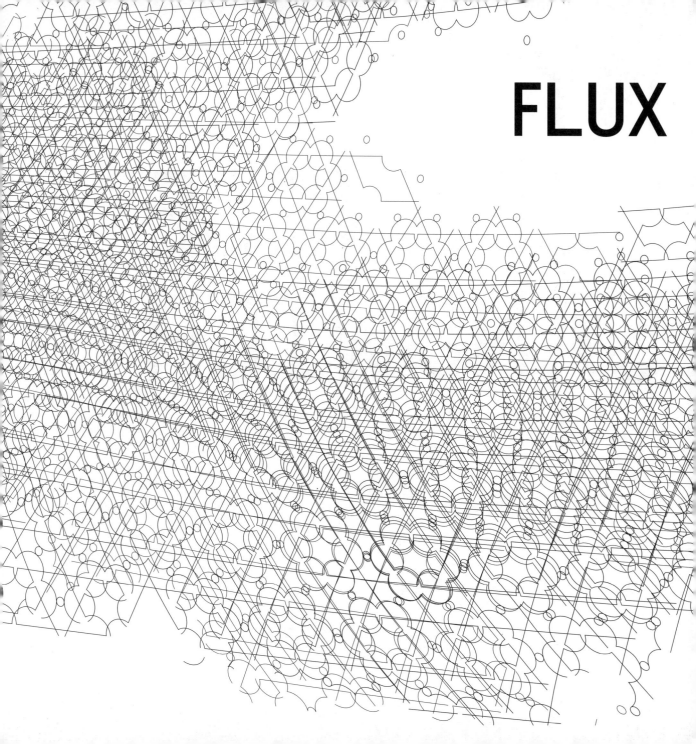

FLUX

MY LEBANESE SANDWICH

Maher Kassar and Ziad Halwani

I'm in Moscow airport, waiting for the weekly flight back to Beirut. People know each other on this flight. There are the same familiar faces: businessmen, escort girls and pimps. While having a snack before boarding – and happily saying goodbye to what seems to be staple Russian airport food: rye bread, mayonnaise and *kalbasa* sausage – I hear a voice in Arabic asking me: 'Did you have fun in Russia?' Moussa is from Jounieh. He is one of the few tourists to whom a travel agency sold an 'all in' package deal to Russia, including food, hotel in Moscow, and guaranteed female entertainment. He seems totally disoriented and out of place here. He asks for my help and follows me from the restaurant all the way through the long formalities of the Sheremetyevo airport. He tells me his holiday was a nightmare. Nothing was as promised. The three-star hotel had no hot water, and everything is so expensive in Moscow. And the food, my God the FOOD!!! The girls were alright but they were not allowed in the hotel after midnight. The third day, he fled to Minsk, to some friend's place. There, he went to the local market, bought meat and vegetables and cooked his own food. This at least allowed him to survive the rest of the trip. 'All this time,' he says, 'I was dreaming of a *falafel* sandwich.' Moussa went to Russia with a hunger for young, beautiful blondes; he came back with an even bigger hunger for *falafel*.

As he said goodbye and cheerfully thanked me, I felt a growing uneasiness. Something was not right about his story. Usually when you leave for a long period and miss the taste of the food of your country, you are – so to speak – home-food-sick not fast-food-sick. Why would he choose to miss the taste of *falafel* when he could pick from a plethora of succulent, typical Lebanese home-cooked dishes? Vine-leaf rolls stuffed with rice and minced meat, and cooked with lamb's tongue. *Mloukhieh,* a delicate green broth mixed with rice, chicken, lamb, toasted bread, lemon sauce and vinegar sauce. (This is my favourite because it is a 'living' dish; you keep adding each of the ingredients, slightly changing the taste every time, keeping your plate full and alive for as long as you wish.) Or *samakhe harra,* an oven-baked white fish with a rich and spicy sesame oil sauce topped with grilled almonds and pine nuts. And these are the obvious ones. Did this man have no taste? He seemed to be one of us though; I mean the kind who cares a lot about food.

This encounter made me reflect on the particular affection the Lebanese have for their fast food. I started remembering all those happy faces biting into *shawarma,* satisfied and content. I remembered the expectation in their glittering eyes as the sandwich man adds the salad, the onion, the *taratór* (tahini sauce) and the pickles before finally wrapping the sandwich and solemnly handing it to them: 'One *shishtaouk,* one!'

But, what makes it so special? Why does it have such a strong hold on the Lebanese heart – something to miss when you're abroad? After all, it is only fast food. And I wonder: can the same pleasure be obtained from eating a Big Mac?

.BIG, FAT AND UGLY … IT'S FAST FOOD ALL RIGHT!

First things first. Let's identify our subject of interest: *shawarma, falafel, shishtaouk,* Armenian *soujouk* and *bastirma,* and bakery products such as *manouché lahmbajin, ftaye* and *kaak.*

.THE LEBANESE MOTHER

In Lebanon it is no easy job to leave the family home and even more difficult to leave your mother's cooking. Chances are you will be eating, at the same table and at the same assigned place, the same fifteen to twenty traditional recipes – however wonderfully executed – for a good part of your life. The road to independence out of the household is long and full of ambushes.

It is not conceivable, for example, that you leave without being married. Your first mission is to find a proper bride from a respectable family. It is also highly recommended that she be from the same religion since only religious marriages are recognized in our country. However, if you are a free spirit looking for further complications and unwilling to give up on the beautiful candidates that the other seventeen communities have to offer, you will have to plan (and pay for) a civil marriage abroad, usually in Cyprus. Or you dig deep into the other solution that requires a conversion to the other belief. However, by the time both the religious authorities and the families are won over, and all the 'details' are settled, you will both be eager to divorce.

Now, let's say you have found someone. You will only be considered a proper party for marriage if you have the housing issue settled. Yes, you'd better own a house. Don't think you're going to take our daughter and live on the streets … Of course, you can rent or buy a small apartment, but if you're a good man and you're as serious as you pretend to be, it is advisable that you build a house from scratch. You'd better find an architect, a contractor, bricks, concrete, land, and the cash. No wonder there's so little free space in Lebanon. Imagine if every male soul with a crush on someone finds a piece of land and starts laying bricks.

Many of my friends have tried to escape the whole process; and although most of them were definitely James Dean material, they were quite unsuccessful. You could try to go on your own, try to cut the umbilical cord prematurely, be a rebel and do the crazy thing. You might be broke for a while, fight to pay your rent and lead a frugal existence. But don't worry, you will never be hungry. Mama will always be there for you. She will visit every week with stacks and stacks of Tupperware with enough home-cooked food to feed you and all your friends until the day you decide to be a reasonable young man again and come back home where you belong; whenever that day might be. Of course, you can try to hide and not disclose your new address. But Lebanon is a small country. She will find you.

If you follow all this advice, you have a chance to break free one day. You will decide where you prefer to sit at the table, what food you would like to eat, and who knows, you might even want to have a shot at cooking yourself. But nothing is guaranteed. If your parents have a little money, there's a good chance they have started the construction of an upper floor for you and your future family. You can already see the unfinished, concrete pillars with the metal rods still sticking out. When more money comes in, they will raise the walls. When it's finished, you can finally get married, my son, and move upstairs.

Then, there will be two rival kitchens competing just to feed you. Your wife will get hell from your mother. First, she will pretend to teach her how to cook. She will give her the recipes just the way you've always liked them. Only for some reason, they will never turn out nearly as good. Too much salt, overcooked, not enough cinnamon. 'Oh, you didn't add lemon, garlic and dried mint on the top? It's true … I forgot to tell you.' Over the years, missing elements of the recipes will be sparingly disclosed. The proportions will eventually correct themselves. But there will always be something missing. Finally, when she has made sure who was the best cook, and is now too tired for kitchen duties, your mother will call for your wife: 'Listen! I am going to tell you what is wrong with your *coussa mehshe*. It is …' The rest nobody else will hear. The secret has been passed on and she, your mother, has made sure that you will be fed the same food. FOR THE REST OF YOUR LIFE.

.THE FREEDOM SANDWICH

You're fourteen, coming out of school with your friends. Something is going to happen. A fact of life. It's your first time. You finally find the courage to go across the street and ask: 'Can I have a *manouché*, please. With tomatoes, olives and a little mint,' you even manage to utter. You hand over your pocket money and timidly take possession of the little thyme pizza.

Yes, congratulations! It is your first meal alone and away from home. And YOU paid for it. Never will you forget the soft and oily dough of the *manouché* in which you sank your teeth for the first time, the tingling, sour taste of the thyme, and the sesame seeds stuck between your teeth. For you, it will always be the taste of freedom and independence, your little secret culinary hideaway from home.

.WORKER'S SIZE

Men at work like to have lunch together. They order sandwiches and start chatting about whatever men like to talk about: business, politics, women, cars … food of course. I believe it is the same everywhere in the world. But in Lebanon, lunch with colleagues is an occasion for very specific male behaviour. At one point, the chatting stops and the munching begins; a collection of impressive jaws bearing down on the defenceless pita sandwiches. Two manly bites and the sandwich is gone, and off we go to the next. It is a silent but fierce competition where all the contenders are required to show their teeth. The bigger the bite, well … I'll let you imagine what's at stake.

In the mid-1990s, in order to answer this growing phenomenon, fast-food joints decided to launch a new product: the Worker's Sandwich. It is really not different from a traditional sandwich, except it's three times bigger. You could get a Worker's *falafel, shawarma, makanik,* or anything you decided to wrap in an oversized pita bread. It really made all those men happy. Armed with their sixteen-inch sandwiches, they could finally parade their manhood.

How much of a man are you, anyway? Go to Abu Ahmad. He will tell you. When you enter the small restaurant and order your sandwich, he will look at you from top to bottom and will make his judgement: 'Two women's *falafel,* two!'

.BARBAR: A SUCCESS STORY

Sandwiches that give you your independence, sandwiches that make you feel like a real man. These are marketing concepts that a Lebanese fast-food owner needs to understand in order to make his business work. But those who make it really big in the extremely competitive world of Lebanese fast food need to have something more, a little spark of genius to stand out from the others; innovation combined with a talent to understand and satisfy the people.

In 1982, Barbar opened in the midst of the civil war. It was a small bakery in the popular area of Hamra, at first solely dedicated to *manouché*: *manouché zaatar*, minced meat *manouché*, *manouché kichk* (a sour dried milk powder) and the traditional *manouché* with runny Bulgarian cheese, except that it was surprisingly topped with sesame seeds. This small innovation was the launch pad for the small bakery of Mohammad Ghaziri, also known as Barbar.

'Have you tried Barbar's sesame and cheese *manouché*?' People started to talk about it and the word of mouth spread like a trail of gunpowder. The fact that it stayed open through the most dramatic days of the war also contributed greatly to Barbar's popularity. 'Twenty-four hours, I'm telling you! They never close.' People recall that it only closed once in honour of two of its employees who were killed in a bombing. Another legend of the Lebanese civil war was born, and the *manouché* bakery took off.

Galvanized by these early successes, Barbar started a wild, ill-defined door-to-door expansion, moving in and occupying every little neighbouring shop whose owner was prepared to surrender.

In a year, the *shawarma* snack bar and the small *falafel* shack opened. Later, following the trend started by the notorious 'King of Vitamin', Barbar opened a fruit cocktail and ice cream shop offering exotic juices such as the Mandela, a chocolate milk shake with banana slices, the Noriega and Castro cocktails, and even the Hitler, a blood-red strawberry cocktail garnished with almonds and pine nuts, topped with whiter than white whipped cream. Finally, a restaurant with seating space, a submarine sandwich joint and a butcher shop completed the Barbar food armada. Soon the little passageway in Hamra became known as Barbar Street and, between the cocktail shop and the sub sandwich restaurant, the street is now blocked by the sign: 'Road Open to Barbar Clients Only'.

Although they are only a few metres apart, every Barbar restaurant has its own kitchen, its own accountancy department and its own employees: a real structural disadvantage due both to the lack of planning and the resolve of remaining shop owners determined to resist Barbar's expansionist plans. The owner of a two-metre wide clock shop, for example, only surrendered half of his small space to Barbar, keeping the other half for himself. One metre of silver watch display still separates the *falafel* shop and the *shawarma*

snack bar. But this is also part of Barbar's charm with its strange, original architecture and its waiters running around the street from one restaurant to the other, shopping for the cocktail, the *falafel* plate and the baked entrées you've ordered while comfortably seated in the restaurant.

Now let's do what everybody has been itching to do. Let's look at the menu. More than 200 items! The Francisco Sub with chicken, corn, mayonnaise and soya sauce was introduced during a period when Beiruti palates began appreciating Asian food. The *Soirée* is another creation. Initially intended to imitate the *petit-four*, it is really like a mini *pirojki* with Lebanese fillings such as minced *shishtaouk* instead of the traditional Russian cabbage or potato. 'Mr Ghaziri travels a lot and brings us all kinds of new food ideas from abroad,' says a Barbar manager when asked about their innovation policy.

Barbar is innovative, but in the vein of some of the politicians after whom Ghaziri has named his cocktails, he is most of all a true populist, taking any food idea and trend that his clients are susceptible to and adapting it to Lebanese tastes. Why go anywhere else? You can find anything and everything at Barbar's: take-away pizza, hamburgers, subs, chicken fried 'Kentucky style', *fajita* sandwich, Chinese chicken, donuts even. You name it, Barbar has it. But everything has been transformed a little bit. The sandwiches and hamburgers have a little more garlic than usual, the pizzas come garnished with *soujouk* or *makanik* sausage, and it is probably the only place in the world where you can order a 'lamb's-brain sub sandwich all dressed'! Even certain names, like the French '*croisson*' on the Barbar's breakfast menu, have been adapted to suit the Lebanese.

But Barbar had bigger dreams and ambitions. He learned from his structural problems and made a plan. In 2001, the new Barbar Spears Street was inaugurated. One long, single space for the *falafel*, the bakery, the *shawarma*, the sub and the take-away restaurants; and a back-door alley for the employees to move freely from one space to the other. At the same time, new competition from foreign fast food forced him to raise his standards. As the Barbar manager explains, 'We have now very strict policies on nail cutting, hand washing and hair hygiene ... what's the word? ... Transparency, yes ... we like our clients to see everything.'

And indeed we see everything that is happening behind the counter; but most of all, we are blinded by the food galore exposed in front of us. From left to right: pickles, lettuce, *taratór, shishtaouk, fajita* chicken, fried fish, fish filet, fried calamari, shrimps, *surimi,* French fries, spicy potatoes, *shawarma* meat, *shawarma* chicken, *makanek, soujouk, bastirma,* lamb's-feet, lamb's-brain ... Along the high-density traffic of Spears Street, a fifty-metre long display of colourful, cold, hot, spicy, exotic meats, salads, fried and baked foods that you are welcome to arrange at will in a sub or pita sandwich.

It's as if the sailboat of Barbar's dreams suddenly materialised in front of us. With its high ceiling, giant posters and blue and pink neon lights visible from far away, Barbar Spears is the Taj Mahal of fast food, the ultimate Lebanese street feeding machine; a model that Barbar is now exporting abroad to the Gulf and other Arab countries.

.THE KING OF KAAK

I never feel as lost, confused and panicked as on Saturday mornings after a night of partying when I open the fridge and realise there is nothing to eat. Hunger grabs me and the urge to fill the empty stomach drives me crazy. I start opening all the drawers and cupboards in the kitchen: a jar of pickles, mustard, Tabasco ... that won't do. I search every corner of the house with frenzy and a growing feeling of desperation. Defeated, I sit on my bed and face reality. I have to dress and leave the house to buy breakfast.

As I drag myself out on to the street and the summer sunrays start warming my body, I feel hopeful again. I know that soon I will come across a *kaak* vendor pedalling in the opposite direction. '*Kaak*! *Kaak*!' the young man shouts. On a wooden frame on the back of his old bicycle, the sesame topped, crescent-shaped *galettes* are hung in several rows. As he lifts the plastic sheets protecting the *kaak,* I try to decide on the filling: *Zaatar* or *picon*? I choose *picon,* the 'Famous French cream cheese' found only in Lebanon. 'Thank god for the *kaak* street vendors!' That's all I can think as I bite into the crispy golden *kaak* envelope stuffed with the soft cheese.

For as long as I can remember, there have been *kaak* vendors in Beirut. Hundreds of street carts and bicycles patrolling the streets of the city in search of ravenous souls like mine. They are a gift, or better, a public service; always there when you need them. For 750 LL or fifty cents, you can fill your stomach and satisfy cruel hunger.

Abu Ali with the cash and the Kaak

'Where do all these *kaaks* come from anyway?' Without hesitation, the seller answers, 'Abu Ali.' When I ask him where I can find this man, he tells me to go further up the line of vendors and ask again, saying, 'They will surely know.' Slowly, I work my way up from Gemmayze to Basta; and with every *kaak* vendor that I meet, I am greeted with the same answer: 'Abu Ali? Of course! Go further up and ask. Everybody knows Abu Ali.'

In the narrow streets of Basta, I follow the trails that lead to the bakery of Abu Ali. Vendors with empty carts accompany me through the traffic. From the opposite direction, those loaded with fresh *kaak* start singing the calls that they have repeated relentlessly for years: '*Kaak* for the morning, *kaak* for the evening.' '*Kaak*, *kaak*, buy my *kaak*.' The cycle of nasal, high-pitched voices is a lullaby that seems to carry the strong smells of freshly baked *galette* and toasted sesame.

Further up the street, as the concentration of people, voices and smells becomes thicker, workers are unloading enormous bags of flour from a big truck. I realize that I have arrived. The place is small and humble. No door, no windows, just a few steps separate the street from the single space oven. As I start my way up, a young man instantly blocks the entrance and asks me: 'Yes? What do you want?' 'I … I'm a reporter doing an article on *kaak*. I would like to meet Abu Ali.' As he lets me in, I feel privileged.

I have no difficulty recognizing Abu Ali. He is an old man, and his authority over the young workers, and everybody else around, is unmistakable. The place is busy and he controls the operations. 'Go wash your hands,' he orders one of his employees. 'What are you doing? Not here! Get a brain!' he blasts the exhausted hauler whose body is nearly collapsing under a bag of flour three times his weight. Even to his sole clients, the *kaak* vendors, he is unremittingly tough, never stepping down from the heights of his bakery and never letting them up the stairs.

With me, however, he is extremely charming. He smiles and tells me everything I want to know: he's been working in the business since 1957. Before that his father and grandfather owned a *kaak* bakery in the old downtown. His sons, however, will not succeed him. 'They are all doctors, engineers or something like that.' He says it so sadly that he makes me feel like taking over myself.

He tells me about the dark days of *kaak*, during the 1990s when people used to associate *kaak* vendors with Syrian intelligence. In response he decided to paint the red and white Lebanese colours and the national cedar tree on the walls of the bakery. Many *kaak* vendors also pin Lebanese flags on their carts to show their patriotism. He tells me about his business and projects. He produces up to 6,000 *kaaks* a day and has just signed a contract to deliver mini-*kaaks* to Middle East Airlines for their early breakfast flight.

When the interview is over, he carefully chooses a piece of *kaak* from the racks near the oven. With his thumb, he makes a hole in it and fills it with his personal thyme mix (*zaatar*) which he keeps hidden under a table. 'This one's for you,' he says. Slowly, he lights a Cuban cigar and waves to me to come and sit outside next to him. 'I love cigars but I never smoke after 2.00 PM. At my age, I have to be careful!'

Sitting on his plastic chair outside the bakery, cash in one hand and cigar in the other, Abu Ali lords it over the street and all the *kaak* vendors. He has succeeded, in authentic Lebanese style.

.THE RISE AND FALL OF THE MAC
I will never forget the surreal scenery of Ain al-Mraisse during Ramadan. It is 4.30 in the November afternoon and the sun is setting in beautiful colours that seem to say: we're not in Europe, we're not in Asia, we're in the middle. The place, usually overcrowded with pedestrians, is totally deserted. People have answered the call of the *muezzin* announcing the end of the fast. In this still and ethereal atmosphere, the voice seems to envelope everything around it: the palm trees standing at the beginning of the Corniche, the mosque on the other side of the street and in between, sticking out with its bright red and yellow colours, the two-storey McDonald's restaurant.

During the war, people dreamt of having a McDonald's in Beirut. They considered that it would be a sign that civilization had finally reached us. The notorious 'M' sign was copied and used by several fast-food establishments. 'M' stood for Massis, the renowned Armenian fast-food restaurant with its exquisite *soujouk* sandwiches and famous 'Odour-free *Bastirma*'. We even had our own 'McDonald's' though its mascot was not Ronald, the ever-smiling clown, but Donald the Duck. It was as close to civilization as we could get.

Civilization … We asked for it and we got it, big time. Along with the new roads, the new infrastructure, the new international airport, a brand new downtown, cellular phone networks, satellite TV, superstar European DJs and modern beach resorts, the thirteen-year-long effort to reconstruct Lebanon after the war lead to the opening of 9 McDonald's, 8 Burger Kings, 4 KFCs, 11 Starbucks, 6 Dunkin Donuts, 1 TGI Fridays and 8 Pizza Huts. And for a little while, everybody was happy. While buying our children a Happy Meal, we had the impression that 'Lebanon (was) moving toward better days' – as McDonald's Lebanese franchise owner Jean Zoghzoghi puts it; and of course the international fast-food chain executives were happy to find another four million healthy bellies willing to be filled.

But this golden period was not meant to last. Like a new toy, the Lebanese played with the Whopper, tried the McFlurry and collected all the buttons and badges from TGI Fridays. Today, the hype is gone and the spirit of our good old *falafel* and *shawarma* is back.

A friend once told me that what she loved about McDonald's is that wherever you go in the world, you can be assured of getting the same quality and the same taste. In other words: everybody is equal in savours and flavours. This is the strength of the Big Mac. And this is precisely why it will fail here in Lebanon. Listen carefully, Ronald McDonald: we do not want to be standard. We want to be an exception. We do not want to be treated like everybody else. We want to be special. When we order a sandwich, we ask the chef to prepare it '*Alla zawaak*' (to his own taste). I want him to look at me, guess how much *taratór*, how much onion and tomato would suit my palate. I want a sandwich tailor-made for me. 'This *falafel* sandwich, Mr Kassar, is just for you. Nobody else in the world has eaten one like this, I can assure you.'

And then there's the politics. At the beginning of the second Intifada in September 2000, a campaign was launched in Lebanon and other Arab countries to boycott US goods. 'The penny you spend buying these products amounts to another bullet for the body of our brave Palestinian brother,' the leaflet said in reference to the three billion dollars a year of direct US aid to Israel. In April 2002, after the six-week Israeli offensive in the West Bank and the forced confinement of Arafat in his Ramallah headquarters, the fast-food boycott took on another dimension. Students in Beirut organized sit-ins at Burger King, Starbucks and McDonald's. Tragically, bombs were planted at Pizza Hut, KFC and McDonald's, resulting in the injury of a teenage girl and significant property damage.

.McARABIA

But global companies don't go down without a fight. To regain public sympathy, targeted marketing campaigns were launched. Coca-Cola began planting cedar trees in the southern Lebanese town of Jezzine and has recently sponsored the Palestinian national soccer team. On the culinary front, Burger King and McDonald's decided to market new sandwiches. Last year, the Kafta King and the McKafta were the stars of the summer season. More recently, the streets of Beirut were covered with giant posters of the brand new McArabia.

I have taken it upon myself to try the McArabia for you. I have allowed my bag to be searched at the door of McDonald's and undergone the shame of having to loudly pronounce the words: 'One McArabia, please.' Would a Swedish person accept asking for a 'McScandinavia' or worse, a Frenchman order a 'McFrance'? But what the hell, I'm an 'Arabian' after all, so I pronounced the magic words and I received, in reward, my sandwich.

On the back of the closed cardboard box, a small cartoon demonstrated the correct procedure for opening the package and the most convenient way to hold the sandwich. I am now in the 'Ready-to-Eat' position and I can finally bite two slices of chicken burger wrapped in a Mcversion of pita bread with shredded lettuce and tomato, topped with a light mayonnaise-like sauce.

My verdict is immediate: bland, gummy … culturally neutral chicken. Culturally neutral! I feel like I've just bitten into one of those yellow Afghan aid packages specially designed not to hurt the Afghanis' religious feelings. They also had a cartoon explaining how to eat the food, as well as an American flag, to make sure that there was no misunderstanding the identity of the benefactor.

But there was a more serious flaw. There is no garlic in the Arabian sandwich! It only struck me later when I realized that I had none of the garlic-related inconveniences, which I usually experience after eating a Lebanese sandwich. We put garlic sauce everywhere, and two layers rather than one. It's called 'Garlic extra!'

In the Beirut sandwich hall of fame, the chicken garlic and pickles *panini* from Marrouche is first with no contest. A friend of mine who used to live off it when she was a student and has now become a vegetarian – another one lost to the cause – could not completely abandon the intrinsic taste of the Marrouche sandwich. She now orders a 'chicken sandwich, garlic extra, without chicken … thank you!'

But I have no illusions. I know that garlic is a forbidden ingredient at McDonald's. Bad breath is not part of their image. They cannot afford the bad publicity of someone kissing his girlfriend and her saying, 'You! You have just eaten a McArabia.' KFC is more accommodating. They understand our attachment to garlic, especially with chicken. If you ask for it discretely, they will hand you one or two cups of garlic sauce under the counter. But, shhhh, don't tell a soul!

.ANGRY STOMACHS, ANGRY ARABS

It's not because Palestinian territories have been reoccupied, or that Arafat is confined to his Ramallah headquarters – miles away from the nearest *falafel* shop – that Burger King and McDonald's are falling out of fashion in Lebanon. Let's, for once, not put the blame on the Israelis or the Palestinians. Let's be honest with ourselves.

It is our stomachs. They are unsatisfied, and they are the culprits. Not enough taste, not enough garlic is the reason why we boycott, organize sit-ins and throw stones. If the surest way to an Arab's heart is his stomach then don't mess with it. War has been declared on the culinary front and the guard at McDonald's is not searching your bag for dynamite, a gun or a knife. He is looking for the illicit garlic sauce, our own homemade chemical weapon. So, please, for the sake of peace, start making better-tasting sandwiches!

THE MOUSE, THE VISITOR AND THE MAN WHO WAS KILLED WEARING MY CLOTHES

Rachid El Daif

My guest ruined the whole evening for me. Soon after she arrived, she went to the bathroom, where she killed a mouse without my help – in fact, without my being aware of a thing, apart from a brief muffled sound in the bathroom. But what had caused it? I had no idea at the time.

'I've killed a mouse for you,' she told me when she came back to the sitting-room.

'For me!' I said. 'For *me*?' I sat bolt upright as if I'd just been stung by a scorpion hidden in a corner of the sofa, and promptly sent the candle I was using to light the room, flying. This seemed to put my guest on edge.

'Weird!'

I decided there and then that she wasn't staying the night after that, however rude it might seem of me. (I'd been pressuring her so much to come round that she'd had to use every trick in the book to convince her parents to let her sleep over 'at a girlfriend's place'.) As luck would have it, it was still early and the situation in Beirut was relatively calm. There was nothing going on – no kidnappings or fighting or anything, just the odd exchange of gunfire over the Green Line. So I asked her to get out. When she insisted that I tell her why, I fetched the morning's paper, brought it close to the candle and told her to take a good look at a photo on one of the inside pages.

'You see this dead guy?' I said to her. 'He's the one who was a squatter in my flat, up until yesterday, when he got killed!'

My guest seemed more unnerved at this and took a few steps back. 'How do you know it was him?' she asked.

'Look at the pale leather jacket he's wearing,' I told her. 'Look at the cut and the buttons on it. And look at the shoes he's got on – there aren't any clothes like that anywhere in Lebanon. Don't they ring a bell? Isn't that the same jacket you advised me to buy at that shop down by the AUB Hospital, off Hamra Street? Don't you remember how you told me it looked great, that it "really suited me", and how it was a bargain, too? And those shoes – they're unique. My brother sent them to me from California after I'd had them specially made. It was after I'd been hit by shrapnel from a missile and had to have a nerve graft in France to restore the movement to my shoulder and one of my hands. The surgeon took half a metre of nerve from one of my legs to connect my neck and shoulder again. The result was that I lost all feeling in my foot. So then I had to start wearing special shoes. Look at them! Look what thick soles they've got, and how low the heels are!'

When I woke up this morning, I went straight out to buy the paper before I'd even had breakfast, as if someone was urging me on somehow. When I set eyes on that picture I thought I'd gone out of my mind. 'Rachid,' I said to myself, 'it looks like this is your lucky day! Go and get your flat back – the guy who was squatting there's been killed!'

I took a taxi to Beirut, pronto. When I got to my flat, I opened the door without any problem – that guy was so sure of himself he hadn't even bothered to change the lock! He obviously wasn't expecting some little pussycat like me to come bothering him. And he was right: the only thing I'd done after I heard he was squatting in my place (I'd gone to stay with my family for a few days) was to try and find someone who could talk some sense into him for me. But now that I was really, truly back in my own home, after a whole month away, I was overjoyed – I felt stronger than I'd ever felt before. I started walking round the place. That guy had clearly been using it to get together with his girlfriends. There were signs of their little rendezvous everywhere. But there couldn't have been anyone else staying there, because only one of the beds had been slept in. Then I found what I'd been looking for, the Kalashnikov! No one would be a better shot than me after this. I felt stronger than the whole Red Army put together, like I'd be able to defeat it, single-handed! What bastard would dare try forcing me out of my home now?

By the time my guest arrived I had the place so clean it was gleaming like a mirror, as my mother used to say. So where did that mouse come from, to spoil my evening? And why didn't my visitor call me to come and help? Why didn't she scream? I'd have come running to the rescue, or at least offered a bit of moral support. Aren't I even up to helping a woman kill a mouse any more?

So I threw her out.

I snuffed out the candle, put the Kalashnikov down beside me and waited. I'd be a fool not to think I might have made a mistake.

'Maybe it would be a good idea to go and offer the guy's family my condolences,' I said to myself just before I dozed off. 'Just to put my mind at rest – they'll assume I'm one of his friends and won't think anything of it. At least that way I'll be able to make sure it was him who was really killed, for good.

Translated from French by Robin Bray

THE CONQUEROR OF THE DOLLAR

Hasan Daoud

On street banners, the man whose name is Muhammad Rahhal appears to have added his father's given name to his own, thus becoming Muhammad Mustafa Rahhal. Here, in the office where we work, not a single colleague knows who he is. And when we began to ask around, everyone we met frowned and offered no information at all. People seemed startled by our question, even though the signs bearing this man's name and slogans appeared in many of Beirut's streets. On banners in Quraytam, he offered his felicitations on the occasion of Lebanon's Independence Day, and expressed the hope that when the next one rolled around, the country would be truly independent because Israel would have withdrawn from the south. On other banners around Hamra, he hailed President Hafez al-Assad. On Army Day, he seized the opportunity to wish the army well – or rather, the two armies, Lebanese and Syrian, on the coincidental convergence of their annual national holidays.

When we asked about him, no one knew him despite the banners at the intersection which all of us passed daily and could not avoid seeing. 'Muhammad Mustafa Rahhal,' we took to repeating, but sometimes we said just plain 'Muhammad Rahhal', without his father's name. That's because when he first started to publicize his name, he used the shorter version to which he added, at the end, *Qahir al-dullaar* (Conqueror of the Dollar).

'Muhammad-Rahhal-Conqueror-of-the-Dollar' had been written on banners for several years now and broadcast on the radio during commercial breaks. As to the question of why he conquered it, that could only be explained by another morsel of information gleaned from a banner or a radio spot, about Galerie Muhammad Rahhal.

Never before on his banners and posters had he revealed himself so fully. Matter of fact, he had left it to the Lebanese people to collect miscellaneous bits of news in order to form a complete picture of him and his line of work. If the names Muhammad and Rahhal that were broadcast on special occasions and in advertisements all referred to the same person, then he was the proprietor of a commercial establishment for home furnishings, Galerie Muhammad Rahhal, which set its prices low ('Conqueror of the Dollar'). But this year he added another dimension to his name, and that's how it showed up on the latest banners: 'Muhammad Mustafa Rahhal and His Supporters'. Just like that, with no explanation, it would lead an observer to assume that he had pulled out of the home furnishings business and had turned instead to public service. For why would the owner of a Galerie need supporters, and what did he hope to gain from them? As a matter of fact, they probably would have hampered his business by crowding into the Galerie.

They might even scare away customers, who would not come in if they saw the Galerie looking like an election headquarters on voting day.

Actually he should have maintained his ownership of the Galerie and allocated himself to both pursuits, acting like a merchant here and a popular leader there. But had he done this, his supporters would be barred from going to the Galerie. But then where would they gather? The office mates here had not seen them gathering. That is, none of my colleagues had seen a gathering of the supporters of Muhammad Rahhal.

Supporters, no one saw. But perhaps they were waiting at home until it was time to congregate? Not to raise a ruckus of course, but for the sake of exchanging congratulations and felicitations, which might raise Rue Hamra above its crass commercial character. And one of the harbingers of this development was that the tradesman Muhammad Rahhal had conquered the competition on the street by elevating himself to the stature of the military forces who, despite their courage, have found no good alternative to gathering adherents for their own protection.

PLACE DES MARTYRS

Antoine Boulad

At a time when the republic is threatened, when the country is in danger of breaking up and disappearing, evoking Place des Martyrs inevitably brings on a kind of painful nostalgia. It breaks my heart and tears my consciousness apart. This square used to bring together things that now seem irreconcilable. Travellers going to every corner of Lebanon left from this square; wayfarers from the four corners of the country ended their journeys here. Muslims, Christians, Jews, Armenians, Kurds, Arabs, westerners and Orientals, rich and poor, men and women, came to this alchemist's crucible to share their sweat, their hopes, their material worries and their spiritual concerns, in effect creating our identity.

Everything began and ended in the city centre. That was why it was the civil war's primordial theatre. A country shatters when its capital is wounded, like a point and a circumference; a capital disintegrates when its city centre is destroyed, the two concentric circles make a nation. Or unmake it. And the men of tomorrow will be able to do no more than dance in the ruins.

They will never confidently entrust their hairy throats to Mr Rizk Saroufim who, for twenty-five years, had his barber shop beneath the steps of the Café de l'Orient. It was one square metre. The pride of place was taken by his diploma from Paris. In the midst of the anthropological-looking mechanical clippers and the out-of-date magazines, it hung between the blades of a struggling fan and a washbasin that was losing its enamel, between the outrageously modern telephone and tall mirrors that had gone yellow around the edges. The customers were as dated as the magazines they flicked through on the bit of pavement outside that served as a waiting-room.

Like all barbers, he was talkative and philosophical. He used to say: 'When they're in my chair, the big – meaning senior civil servants – and the little are equal.' And who would dare to contradict a man who was holding the sharp blade of a guillotine over his manly head?

Like all good barbers, he was also the official keeper of rumours that circulated in the area. He carefully filed them on the shelves and in the whorls of his ample brain. 'Hasn't your sister just become the lawful wedded wife of Abdel-Rahma?' He would ask. And then, should an unexpected gap in your memory prevent you from replying, the frenetic snip-snip of the scissors he wielded with such dexterity would come dangerously close to your ears. Shamefully, the scissors were responsible for loosening your tongue!

They will never go, at any hour of the day or night, to the lemonade stalls or the hanging gardens around the Souk Ayas. The gardens overflowed with the fruits of the earth. They will never suck the velvety mangoes, nor the bluish earth of the orange. They will never sip the groundswell of sugar-cane or the ravine of the guavas. They will never whisper the canticle of mandarins in their throats, nor distil the fire of pomegranates in their veins or the foam of a grapefruit. They will never succumb to the thrust of bananas, the hailstones of strawberries, or the sultry charm of liquorice. And they will never watch in wonder as a swan glides across the lake, and swallow the last drops of *jellab*, with its pine kernels, its raisins as dry as pebbles, and its almonds as sweet as kisses.

They will never hear time stand still in the Café de la République where the bird sellers, who were always there to set their narghiles chirping by blowing the few cares they had into a kind of tube. So they will never know this idle race, time's glass blowers, who keep one peaceful eye on important things. A narghile is better than a cigarette because it brings together the four elements: fire in the form of glowing charcoal, as the little boy swings his censer, water cooling in the curve of a pipe, air to revive it with a horde of wild bubbles. And the earth on which the narghile stands connected to the soul by a metaphorical umbilical cord.

Then there were the dice players who would spit out a litany of swear-words and make a gallant last stand, depending on whether luck was with or against them. The ticking of clocks mingled with the clicking of the backgammon pieces, overturned ashtrays and hours punctuated by strings of insults. Sometimes their plain-speaking was studded with the latest news about the country's political situation. They disseminated the most truthful stories from the highest of sources, invented the propitious information they lacked without any fear of being contradicted, or talked ironically about the latest wonders of science.

They will never get themselves as lost in the Grand Theatre's Umayyad arcades during the first days of October. Or in the inextricable human tangle that emerges when the schools let out an army of hard-working schoolboys, an ant hill of brats, accompanied by their tutors, most of them illiterate, bawling out the titles of battered classics and auctioning them off as if they were sacks of common garden potatoes. They rummaged through the tiny bookshops, where the whole world's culture was piled high and sold cheap by stallholders who, buzzing, gesticulating and dripping with sweat, could scarcely make out the learned titles. And then later during the school year, when their pocket money ran low, they would sell their old copy of *Le Cid* for a handful of piastres in order to buy pizza for their girlfriends after the Saturday night movie.

They will never encounter in the labyrinths of Nourieh the gangs of porters, most of them young kids who, apart from helping ladies by carrying their bulky purchases in the baskets on their backs, or by selling them strong paper bags, tripped passers-by or splashed them by paddling in the nauseating mixture of water and blood that ran in the ancient gutters of the cobbled streets. Then the young kids ran off as fast as they could, slipping like eels through the vaulted passages until they reached the stinking fish market, and disappeared from sight.

After a hard day's work, these rascals would usually end up in the depths of the Venus Cinema, which ran pornographic films sleazy enough to get them breathing heavily until they fell asleep like good little hoodlums.

They will never be cheated by the thieves of Azarieh, who would have gotten them to place heavy bets on a little ball – a volatile ball – supposedly hidden under a thimble. There would have been lookouts posted on the street to warn against the unexpected arrival of policemen.

I remember my friend André who had just been given the fabulous sum of 700 pounds by his father to pay his school fees. We were returning late at night from Achrafiye and were planning to spend the night in Mousaitba and to do this we had to walk across the Green Line to reach West Beirut, a zone which was to become a battlefield a few years later. We were too young to grasp the future, too clear-sighted to see that our night-time walk was taking us along a line that would eventually tear the nation apart.

As we passed the imposing Azarieh shopping centre, we were drawn like magnets to a gathering of people. 'Place your bets,' shouted a hirsute young man. He was using a battered cardboard box as a casino. We placed our bets and that was that. Our pockets emptied like pearls falling off a bracelet. We were supposed to guess which of the three thimbles was hiding the tiny silver ball. If we guessed right, we would win twice our stake – hundreds of pounds of notes. From time to time, the thuggish high priest allowed his accomplices to win, so as to not arouse our suspicions. It was not until several months later that we learned – we were actually told by one of these arrogant rogues who plagued the city centre – how the trick worked: the ball we were shown before we made our bets magically vanished under a disproportionately long finger nail. The punters were betting on something that wasn't there.

Even today, I still feel some remorse. I feel ill at ease at having been careless enough to lead my friend into that den of thieves. I can no longer remember how André managed to pay his school fees, but neither of us dreamed of blaming the con men at the time. I've even asked myself whether we didn't feel some sympathy for them.

This perimeter is now off limits to a whole generation of Lebanese. For us, the Place des Martyrs and the surrounding areas where we spent our youth in a cold sweat was a field of possibilities, one in which we made our début in life, the place where we tasted freedom.

I used to wander through the alleys of the city centre, carried away by the crowd, sharing the destiny of men, breathing in its smells and colours, while at the same time experiencing a sort of loneliness. I would melt into the crowd, but my main preoccupation was with myself. Although I certainly shared their fate by dressing poorly and trying to look the part, I kept a philosophical distance from the crowd. The reason why I loved the sweat of men and the smell of fried fish in those narrow alleyways, where I had to elbow my way through, probably a place that other people avoided like the plague, was because all of this sustained and nourished my poetic soul. The reason why I loved the music that blared out from the juke boxes and the radios – Abdel Halim Hafez was popular at the time, with his songs that dripped love – is that I was soaking in the exoticism, savouring my own country like some wide-eyed foreigner.

I can still hear the sound of my heels on the cobblestones of the red light districts to the right of the square as I walked towards the port, following its meanders and capillaries, drawn by the mysteries of the night and femininity. I went there so many times. I idled away the hours in those places, intrigued by every being and every object. I was on the lookout for things that never change and for anything furtive. I caressed the smells, taking an anguished delight in the swishing of the coloured reed curtains that singled out the doors of the bars.

When Lebanon recovers from its fragmentation, let the city centre be rebuilt, and let talented engineers and zealous architects design its lines and forms. But please God, let the subterranean world that opened up before my greedy eyes inspire them. Let it rise from its ashes, and let them build homes for the prostitutes from the Black Cat and all the other bars.

Antoine Boulad's essay 'Place des Martyrs' was included in *Atazakkar, Fractions of Memory*, a public art installation by the artist Nada Sehnaoui, from 1 July to 31 August 2003. The essay was translated from French by David Macey.

THE GARDEN OF THE TWO MARTYRS

Fadi Tufayli

Photos by Dalia Khamissy

.ONE

On 15 April 1975, two days after the official date marking the eruption of the Lebanese war, sniper bullets showered down on the Old Sidon Road that bisects Beirut's eastern and western suburbs. The bullets killed two young brothers, Mustafa and Mahdi Hashim, and wounded a third who survived.

The two slain brothers were not taken away for burial in their south Lebanon border village, Rub Thalathin, which would have been the usual practice. Instead, they were carried to the home of some relatives on Marun Misk Street in al-Shayyah, a residential quarter on the outlying western fringes of Beirut, directly across the Green Line from the eastern Christian suburbs. There, the bodies were wound in burial shrouds. The following morning a few neighbours joined the meagre file of pedestrian mourners bearing the brothers to their burial in Beirut's pine woods, Hirj Sanaubar.

The burial rites were performed quickly at the edge of a wooded tract. The hasty, abbreviated ceremony took place just metres from the main road that cuts through Beirut from north to south. This perfectly ordinary road had become, in a matter of days, a line of engagement for the battles flaring between the two opposing sectors of the city.

For all its simplicity, the funeral was not a transitory event that would soon be forgotten. The double burial inaugurated a graveyard, which, a quarter century later, gives fierce expression to the transformations Beirut underwent. Carved in the tranquil pine valley, the two shallow graves were to mark the beginning of the first Shi'ite cemetery on the city's verge, an outer edging that extended towards Beirut as if trying to join it. The brothers' resting-place bequeathed a name to this place: the Garden of the Two Martyrs. It was surely a sign that would augur well; those who named it sought a good omen in the tombs and in the tragic event that created them.

Nothing preceded the graves but trees and a low wall parallel to which the brothers had been carefully buried. Gradually, other graves lined up alongside them to form a row extending northward. Then, to the quickening tempo of combat and events – as the battles piled up on the nearby line of engagement – the graves multiplied. They formed a straight line running all the way from the tombs of the Two Martyrs to the wall at the other end of the valley, which separated the pines from a road constructed through the heart of the woods in the 1960s. Then another line rose parallel to the first, and a third, and then a row perpendicular to the first three. From then on, the graves spread in all directions over the valley of the pines, according to forty-year-old Ali who readied the dead for burial and laid them in their tombs. Ali was heir to the *métier* of his father, who with his own hands, had prepared the two slain brothers for interment in 1975.

Twenty-eight years separate us from that history. Now, the Garden of the Two Martyrs no longer sits on the edge of the city, but has been engulfed by it. Presently the cemetery holds almost five thousand graves. Of that number, only twelve bodies are nameless, wholly unknown to the guards and workers of the garden. These graves have been abandoned: no one visits them; they possess no columnar headstone that would mark them as cherished remains. All the other tombs commemorate the family and lovers of people living somewhere in the vicinity: to the south in the urban periphery, and to the north and west, in Beirut itself. These living relatives – or, at least, most of them – are in constant communication with the resting-places of their departed dear ones.

.TWO

In the nineteenth century, the pine woods were planted to protect the city from the dense winds coming from the south; winds that bore the ferocious sands un-leashed by the excavation of the Suez Canal. At the start of the twentieth century, they held significance for the city that is unimaginable today. Photographs from the period show the wooded area extending outward, with no defined shape or borders. It formed a green rim to the capital's south, which maintained a boundary against the spread of the city and urban construction. The woods separated the two halves of Beirut proper from the activity on the periphery, which remained outside the city's grasping reach.

Narrow lanes crept through the trees to form corridors, which led incomers into Beirut's urban areas, with their interlacing network of streets. The woods acted as a natural crossing, steering the flow of people easily and spontaneously towards the city centre which – prior to the war – had long been celebrated for its extraordinary heterogeneity. And it was Beirut's breathing space, an outlet for the urban population – an ample green circuit free of development that also prevented the rise of potential rivals, localized centres that might diffuse and muddle up the capital's pivotal centre. The woods functioned as a primitive dam of branches and plants that contained the rushing waters in a lake from which they could be channelled into manageable streams.

In the first quarter of the twentieth century, small residential pockets sprang up against the inner edge of the woods. These knots of houses resembled the hamlets spreading along Beirut's shoreline in the same period: small clusters of dwellings settled by working-class people who depended on local resources for their livelihoods. The people of Ain al-Mraisse, the seaside neighbourhood on the city's south-western shoreline, focused their energies on the sea by running seafood stores, fishing or working in the nearby Beirut Harbour. Meanwhile the residents of Hayy al-Arab – 'Arab' being the name of a family from the area abutting the pine forest – found employment from the woods. In a place of shaded and undisturbed re-creation, the people of Hayy al-Arab put up small stands for selling all sorts of products to those who ambled by. They erected swings on feast days and earned their bread as guides for people walking towards Beirut. They took outsiders to the markets and other

destinations all over the city. Some became intermediaries in negotiations between the newcomers and merchants in the *souks*. However, these developments did not alter the essential character and function of the forest.

The Garden of the Two Martyrs was one of the first signs that the environmental barrier between Beirut and its periphery had been breached. It was an early indication of a radical overturning. Patterns and flows, crossings and transits came about which drew – and finally brought together – elements that had previously been kept apart. Without the war, the same would have happened, but it would have followed other paths, taken different forms.

Before the conflict, a key element in the bond linking the rural migrants pouring into the cities to their country origins was the continued practice of burying their dead where they had been born. People maintained contact with their native villages through periodic visits to family graves. The dislocation of the war made it absolutely necessary for them to find an alternative and more practical solution for burying their dead. As the hostilities stretched on, the temporary site of the Garden of the Two Martyrs began to assume a permanent form, which would have an impact on many levels. It not only influenced an elemental aspect of families' ties to their rural birthplaces in south Lebanon or the Bekaa plains to the east, but also affected residential patterns on the city's southern periphery.

The interminable years of strife forced those who had fled to the urban fringe to become permanent residents of their overcrowded neighbourhoods, areas that grew haphazardly, without the benefit of planning. And the Garden of the Two Martyrs cemetery gave added impetus to their continuing presence. For not only did the cemetery breach the barrier between Beirut and its outlying areas to the south, it also played a major part in connecting them. When the woods surrounding the garden were burnt to the ground in 1982 during the Israeli bombing that devastated the city, the extent of the penetration was revealed. With nothing to stop Beirut from extending southwards and meeting the southern fringe creeping towards it, the two advancing areas resembled each other: in colour, in height and in the materials of which they were made. Having consumed all of the available real estate, the individual structures, without any clear pattern or model, form a solitary massive bloc into which are compounded the ingredients of modernity – architecture, consumerism, mass production: cement and gleaming granite, glass, aluminium and nylon.

This meeting blended elements that normally do not come into contact. The buildings and flats of the well-heeled families, who wield political, economic and social clout, mingled with the dwellings of those much lower on the economic and social scale, to the extent that the outer walls, so contrasting in *décor* and patina, press against each other. In time, the area became so overcrowded that the separate districts or neighbourhoods completely disappeared.

The expansion was accelerated by the development of interests and occupations in the quarters around the garden. Dealers in automobile parts and wreckage edged forward from the west. From the east, a scout group attached to a local political party advanced, building a headquarters opposite the first and oldest row of tombs. Proprietors of aluminium and glass manufacturing establishments put up open workshops facing the row of graves to the north, while certain granite dealers exhibited their merchandise along some of the same northern perimeter. These workshops and displays were an active response to the increased demand from entrepreneurial developers erecting new structures nearby: high buildings whose gleaming façades overlook the flat expanse of the unhappy Garden of the Two Martyrs below.

The initial businesses were eventually followed by small factories and little workshops for manual trades; commercial premises and garages; permanent greengrocers and itinerant produce hawkers; and restaurants, welders' noisy forges and showrooms for new and flashy cars – all side by side, as a single mass on a single site.

These disparate components fuse there at the borders of the garden where the smell of death, inescapably piercing one's nostrils, fills the entire area. A real, tangible odour issues from the dissolution of bodies buried in the damp sandy soil, and this, swept up by the winter breezes, floats spider-like through the dense, crowded web of buildings and streets.

.THREE

During the war, contact with the Garden of the Two Martyrs was dictated by the daily rhythm of death. In the late 1980s, when heavy fighting broke out between two major Shi'ite parties, one of them expanded its territory to include the cemetery and the immediate area around it. These clashes, which coincided with an intensification of violent resistance operations against the Israeli army in south Lebanon, swelled the streams of families coming to the garden to bury victims. These events brought the cemetery to its over-populated peak, witnessing on occasion more than ten funeral processions and interments in a single day. The numerous burials and mass building projects necessary to construct enough graves produced a standardized tomb. These were built hurriedly with materials manufactured in the workshops along the garden's edge. Identical materials were used to raise the surrounding buildings and to cover their façades in various patterns and techniques. A fact easy to see when you shift your gaze from the cemetery to the surrounding buildings.

When the battles were at their furnace-like height as the 1980s gave way to the 1990s, one local faction was burying its dead in the Garden of the Two Martyrs while it was under the authority of another opposing faction. These burials took place in silence and under heavy guard, only after obtaining advance temporary agreement from the controlling party. Once that particular internal conflict had come to a close and violence was concentrated in the south of the country, the faction reappeared to tend the graves of its

adherents and to bury new victims who had fallen in the south. Added ceremony made up for previous neglect. In this new phase, the faction honoured the graves of its dead by adding a colourful nylon tent over the tombs, much like the balcony awnings on the surrounding buildings that seemed to blend together to conceal what took place on these balconies or behind them inside the flats.

On the tombs above ground, lustrous granite tiles covered the original cement casing. Engraved into the granite facing were verses from the Qur'an and the name of the deceased. Above that an aluminum and glass box was fixed. It opened with a key and contained photographs of the late lamented one, a copy of the holy book, a rosary, incense and other things used during visits to the tomb, objects cherished both for their metaphysical meaning, and for the domestic life they represented. The materials that went into the adjacent buildings were not so very different. The same cement, granite, aluminium and glass now adorned the façades of all the buildings constructed since the 1980s. The resemblance between the materials adorning the buildings and flats, and those used to embellish the tombs was bizarre and not without a certain bitterness. In the past, the graves had not taken this form and manner of outward show. Or at least, they had not manifested a connectedness to everyday life, now lent to them by the decorative granite tiles and that little glass box, the repository of personal, household items whose key the dead person's family or friends were most carefully preserving.

It is as though these graves had been specially adapted to their new surroundings. The materials of their construction and adornment are intimately connected to the adjacent society and its hurly-burly of political, religious and consumer activities taking place throughout the densely populated network of streets. The connection suggests the extent to which the fabric of life is woven equally from the province of death and the theatre of the living. Because of this, the Garden of the Two Martyrs is no longer a quiet oasis respectful of the dead. Rather, it is a place where the corporeal and the supernatural collide and combine noisily.

At the cemetery's entrance and dotted among its graves, a number of jobbers have positioned themselves, waiting for those who still hope to bury their dead in the garden. They are ready to act as go-betweens. Dispersed throughout the nearby communities, there is a different sort of broker. These wait for customers seeking flats for sale or rent. And so, once again, the economic activity in the cemetery has direct parallels in the localities surrounding it. But with one difference: within the Garden of the Two Martyrs, options are at an absolute minimum. While the real estate brokers accompanying prospective customers to flat after flat, with offers at the ready, have hundreds – not to say thousands – of empty apartments in the recently constructed buildings, the cemetery's overcrowding has led to inflated prices for the few remaining metres of ground. For the newly arriving dead, those with relatives already buried in the garden have

precedence since they can be buried with a brother or father or son in a single pit. Some of the living have reckoned on this by digging abnormally deep graves. That way, an extra place is already reserved for an additional corpse, separated from the first by concrete slats.

There is a sort of stock exchange for grave pricing and burial expenses. The arrangements surrounding death, the business of preparing bodies and selecting the burial sites – all enter into the daily economy of the area. Nylon and the cotton fabric from which burial shrouds are cut, fragrances to scent the water in which the body is washed and different ones later on, as well as other materials used in preparing the corpses, all can be purchased from nearby shops. When added to the fees for the person who prepares the body; the cost of the ceremony, the sermon and the professional mourners; the price of the plot and grave digging; and finally a meal at the end, the total sum might well reach several thousand dollars. Such transactions give death the flavour of the mundane. The material details, merchandising, loud voices, all of which over time have become customary, are as common in the cemetery as they are in ordinary businesses or market-places.

Such dealings yank the late individual's closest relatives out of the mute calm that usually accompanies the event of death. Pulled from imprisoning solitude and grief, they are suddenly propelled into the drama of middlemen and vendors. The necessary encounters push them once again to the stage of local politics. At the entrance to the Garden of the Two Martyrs, above its low metal gate, is a photograph of a local *zaim* who led one of the warring Shi'ite parties. It is a large photograph, in colour of the smiling leader, signifying the power and importance of his group. The photograph intimates that anyone entering the cemetery, whether as an individual or part of a group of mourners, must bow their heads and acknowledge an authority, which at least in the garden, is greater than death.

Today, the Garden of the Two Martyrs is stable and unchanging, with the permanence afforded by five thousand graves deep in the soil of Beirut's former woods. It is a gaudy, flashy spectacle of tangled confusion. The past decades of war and the constant flow of emergency migrations towards an already crowded urban periphery now meet on a site which presently marks the centre point between Beirut's two halves, east and west, and the southern periphery, which reached the apex of its development during the war. A densely meaningful representation of the new demographic and architectural changes that have taken place after the war, the scene is peculiarly expressive of the city as a space of separated accumulations. These entities appear as if they have melted together in the heat of battle and political upheaval, agglomerations dissolving into themselves, the weight of each one devouring old discrete components and various miscellanies, whether geographical, architectural, residential or economic. This is a scene before

which one can no longer speak about different areas, temporalities or *milieus* that formerly played an important role in the city's once heterogeneous ways of life. For this is the new Beirut: a single mass, everything resembling everything else, all of it formed in an indifference to time, the most extreme contradictions intertwined within sameness. There no longer exist any agricultural fringes, no summer areas, no woods. Only the sea remains, to the north and west, an ancient sea with a shoreline that erodes further with every day's passage, and a thick, dry, scabrous crust of compacted elements that envelop the surface of the city.

RED
WALLS

Nadine R.L. Touma

First it was the western wall in the living-room.

He painted it red.

A dark red that shines hidden whites when the noon sun hits it.

He emptied the room.

He painted his rocking chair a Mediterranean blue

and put it against the eastern white wall,

facing the western wall.

Then it was the northern wall in the bedroom.

He painted it red.

A dark red that shines hidden oranges when the setting sun hits it.

He emptied the room.

He circled with his wife's red lipstick all the humidity green moulding roses, moons and stars on the western, southern and eastern white walls.

Then it was his son's room.

He painted all the walls red.

A dark red that shines hidden browns when no sun hits it.

He emptied the room.

He undressed himself.

Naked.

He drew a big yellow sun on the floor.

He laid himself in the cold sun and stretched his arms out into his emptiness.

He cried.

He sobbed.

A sun lying in a tired man's womb.

Between him and him,

stretched out on a hospital bed,

in a white robe,

were red circles.

Hundreds of red circles.

He breathed them through his nostrils and took every drop of dark red in.

Nailed to his lips were white eyes that he could close and open,

close and open close and open.

Stop.

Swallow.

Sleep.

Sleep with white eyes in your belly.

He could not close them now.

They were staring at him from the dark red walls.

He could not close them now.

He opened his eyes and ran his red painted hands on his body.

He touched his belly where her head laid open.

Her head lay open with a bullet that cut through the silenced void.

Sunny Sunday afternoon.

He was sitting on her right.

She was sitting on his left.

The kidnapper was sitting on her left.

She was sitting on the kidnapper's right.

His son was sitting on the driver's right.

The driver was sitting on his son's left.

His son was crying.

His hands were on his son's ears.

The wife's left hand was on the husband's mouth.

His angry words biting her scared fingers.

She had her Sunday Yellow Beret on.

She was wearing her Sunday Purple Dress that he had gotten her.

She was heavy with the memories of a night full of love.

And the bullet came out in silence from a muffled gun.

The kidnapper's hand, the trigger, the bullet, her eyes, her eyes in her head,
her head on his lap, his lap in her eyes.

Her head was now rolling in his lap.
Her hand held by a string hanging in the emptiness between him and his son.
Hundreds of red circles hovering over them.
His son did not hear, did not see,
but the red circles tickled everywhere,
the window dripped red circles onto his son's womb.
Sunday Yellow Beret dust sprinkled the air with her perfume.
She always sprayed perfume on her hair.

The driver stopped the car.
The kidnapper threw the man, his wife, her head,
and pieces of Sunday Yellow onto the empty street.
His six-year-old son flew away.

Red circles setting in the horizon.

Everything in him cried.
He licked her.
He loved her.
He rocked her.
He breathed warmth in her mouth.

It was dark outside.
They threw them on the other side of the city.

People in the neighbouring buildings heard endless sobbing moans.
They thought it was a wounded animal.
The sobbing moans were lingering and eternal.
Some people, hiding away from the bombing, started crying.
They did not know why they were crying but they couldn't stop.
A woman opened her window.
She looked in the direction of the deafening hum,
two people embracing.
She yelled, she screamed, she shouted.

One window after another opened unravelling little scared heads

peering out from their holes.

White eyes pinned on darkness.

The sound of the distant bombs could not muffle the sobbing moans.

The yelling of the people increased.

Words that held on to heaven.

A man came out with a red flashlight.

And another man.

And another woman.

Circles of white light encircling the red circles with Sunday Yellow.

No one believed what he or she was seeing so they can start remembering or telling others.

They had already forgotten what they did not see.

They did not know what to ask.

What to say.

The sobbing moans were choking all the staring eyes.

A young man brought his car.

They tried to take the woman in first,

they explained that they were taking them to the hospital,

but the man howled a cry that still resonates in that piece of sky.

(Even years later, if you went to that street, and closed your eyes you could hear it.)

So they had to take them in as one red circle.

They put the broken man, the woman, her head and pieces of Sunday Yellow in the car.

The young man drove with his hand on his horn,

something we usually do at weddings.

The sounds reached the hospital before the car.

They arrived at the hospital.

The red sobbing circle was wheeled in on one white bed.

They could not separate the man from the woman.

He kicked.

He held her head in his arms.

They could not hold him still to inject him with a calming shot.

Finally, one of the nurses whispered something in his ear, held his head against her chest,
the doctor was able to give him the shot.

Everyone in the emergency room was crying.

Even numbed and sedated the husband was still moaning.

No one had ever seen this, in the nine years of war.

The young man tried to explain what had happened.

The young man started crying.

People are supposed to be numb.

Nine years of war.

They separated them.

They undressed her from her beautiful purple dress.

The dress of so many blue seas.

They washed her body.

They wrapped her in a white hospital gown.

They undressed him from the setting suns.

They washed his body from her head.

They put her head on her body.

They wrapped him in a white hospital gown.

Red circles with pieces of yellow flowed on the emergency room's white floor.

Red circles that would eventually flow into the Mediterranean Sea.

Sun ripples of an inexorable shriek.

Yellow pieces that would flow over the sea.
A relentless autumn of fallen heads.

He was still lying on his son's bedroom floor.
In the yellow painted sun.
Three hours later.
Night had fallen on his naked body.
He stood up.
He went to the kitchen, to his man's locker, opened it and got his hammer, nails, and saw.
He went to the room where he had put all the chairs, the tables, the beds, the sofas,
the house.

First he brought in the sofa he grew up with, a wedding gift from his grandmother.
A beautiful 1920s, deep burgundy velvet sofa that still smelled like rose water
from 1960 when he was eleven-years-old. He loved remembering that day.

May of 1960.

It was a hot summer day in his village.

His grandmother had been on the large balcony that was hanging from the sky,

sitting on her low wooden stool, her legs spread out, covered with layers of dresses and aprons, her breasts beautifully expanding into space and embracing his fondling hand. She was everything for him since he had lost his parents in a car accident when he was two.

Like a queen on her throne, she sat there, gently placing the wild mountain purple roses in the copper still. He was sitting next to her, on the stool she had made for him, with his name carved in the walnut wood, one of his hands drowning in her breasts and the other swimming in rose petals. She was making rose water by distilling the flower.

He watched the vapour becoming drops, allowing them to fall in his palm to be picked by his grandmother's tongue: 'Hmmmmm, my soul quencher'. She would say. That day he had felt something strange in his penis every time his grandmother licked his palm. That night, restless, as the whole house was sleeping he went into the kitchen, opened the yellow fridge, poured himself a glass of cold sweetened rose water, went into the special salon where the beautiful burgundy sofa that every nice house in the village had a different version or variation of, was. He ran his fingers across the curves of the sofa, and rested his head on the soft velvet, he felt it again, that same strange feeling in his penis. He put his hand under his cotton white underwear and gently touched himself. He was happy. He dipped one of his hands in the rose water glass and caressed himself with it. The sofa was slipping under him like water. His eyes were closed but he could see a strange light inside him. Suddenly he lost control and dropped the glass of rose water on the special sofa.

He was now breaking the sofa apart. The legs, the arms, the back, the bench. He gently pulled the fabric out and wrapped his waist with a large piece. He felt his grandmother's breasts enveloping him. Warm tears. Warmer. Warmer.

Then he brought in their bed, hers and his, the one they made love in for the first time. When they were students at the university. When he came up to her and asked her if she loved cabbage. When he serenaded her with an accordion concert and fresh walnuts covered with fig jam that his grandmother had made. When their first date was to accompany him to the dentist because he was so scared to go by himself. When she would write him love poems on his bathroom walls with her red lipstick. When they fought because she was going to England to get a doctorate degree and he had to stay in the city, now ravaged by war. When she came back and married him. When they gave birth to their son. When this bed carried the three of them naked in the hot humid summer nights. When it squeaked as they made love and they had to send their son to play in the streets. When they held on to each other holding on to life as bombs were falling around them. When a shrapnel went through the glass of the window above their bed shattered and broken into a million pieces on their son putting him there thinking that it was the safest part of the house and carrying him like a mummified glass creature sleeping from the shock reflecting the lights of the city as they ran to the clinic next door.

He was now breaking the bed apart. The legs, the headboard, the mattress, the sides.

Then he brought in the dining-room table. A rough wooden table.
Cedar wood, of a dead cedar tree that travelled from her northern village to their sea home. They had carved it together, following every vein, leaving some rough areas and smoothing out others, leaving some of the tree's trunk and peeling out the rest, arguing about the shape, and not talking to each other for days until they agreed again and finished it. Two pieces of wood lying on four stones, each a colour, and each with a story and a birthplace, the white stone from the south, the red stone from the west, the sandy stone from the east and the grey stone from the north.

He was now breaking the table apart. The centrepiece cut into smaller pieces.

Then he brought in the dining-room chairs. Each chair was different. They had collected them together over the years, from friends, family, neighbouring countries, antiques sales.

He was now breaking the chairs apart. The legs, the arms, the back, the stool.

Then he brought in his son's bed. By now he was numb. Focused on his desire.

He started putting the pieces of dismembered wood together.
The sun was rising. He had worked non-stop for seven hours. By the time he was finished, it looked beautiful.

He went into the kitchen, blocked the sink faucet, turned the water on and let it run.
He went into the big bathroom, blocked the sink faucet, turned the water on and let it run.
He went into the small bathroom, blocked the sink faucet, turned the water on and let it run.

He went to his turntable and played the Bach cello suites in a volume that shook his being and his inner walls into a dance with ghosts and dreams.

The water was tickling his feet, he was dancing to the music. Jumping and splashing.

Opening the doors to her closet released body aromas that he penetrated with his mouth. He sat inside the closet pulling her dresses down, one by one, as if tearing pieces of paper from an old diary. Falling unto his lap like a bite stuck in his throat exploding into visions of her inside him enveloping all of him and leaving. He breathed her out yet the smell was on his body crawling on him as the water level was rising.

He took a lump of her clothes and allowed them to float freely with the water.

A red dress moving from the living-room to the kitchen

a blue dress floating from the bedroom to the hallway.

A shipwrecked house that the survivor was drowning.

He poured himself a cognac, put Bach from the beginning and went to his beautiful wooden construction,

a tiny boat in which he laid his tired body allowing the water to lullaby him out of this world.

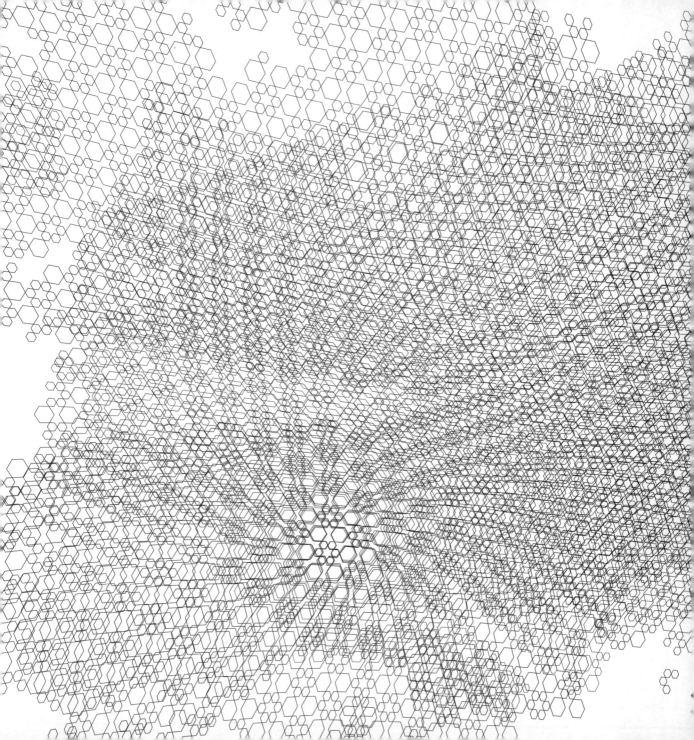

NAVIGATING

LIVING BETWEEN WORLDS

Roseanne Saad Khalaf

I could not live in any of the worlds offered to me ...
I believe one writes because one has to create a
world in which one can live ... I had to create a world
of my own ... in which I could breath, reign, and
recreate myself when destroyed by living.

Anais Nin, *In Favour of the Sensitive Man*

.ONE

We left Beirut in the fall of 1984 with the horror of
war still fresh in our minds. While it was excruciating
to leave family and friends behind, the senseless
battles that raged on in the country only strengthened
our resolve to distance our two young boys from the
savage cruelties of a country torn apart by civil strife.
So many of our friends and acquaintances had become
innocent victims of random violence. Besides, ten
years of barely eking out an existence, of adhering
to the numbing routine of survival was beginning to
take its toll on us. We had been witnesses to every
atrocity imaginable: random shelling, street fighting,
car bombs, sniping, kidnapping, torture, murder and
massacres. Human suffering had reached immeasurable
heights, the brutality was beyond description, and still,
the violence continued to escalate. It was ongoing and
relentless, with no end in sight. Obviously it would be
sheer insanity to take any more chances especially as
we had, on numerous occasions, barely escaped death.
In the darkness of 1984, we finally took the agonizing
decision to leave for what we thought would be a year's
research leave, and I was immediately overwhelmed
with despair. The war had brought so much fear and
sadness to our lives that I was absolutely convinced
we would never be able to shed it all and resume a
normal existence.

In February 1995, after eleven years of involuntary
exile, I found myself back in Beirut. Almost immediately
my sense of place was thrown off balance. This was
not the Lebanon I had come back to in my mind; not
the country I had revisited countless times in my
imagination. Perhaps the Lebanon I had known and
loved had never existed at all. Suddenly I was thrown
into a state of confusion. One thing remained certain,
the surreal atmosphere in the country only served to
heighten my anxieties about this new chapter in my
life. I was shocked by the visual images of a city I
no longer recognized. The chaotic building boom paved
the way for hideous, sprawling housing and commercial
developments. To my horror, fast-food outlets and
kitschy entertainment spots had invaded the Corniche
that hugs a once beautiful and unspoiled seafront.
Concrete monstrosities, unzoned and illegally built
structures now eroded the pristine landscape that
used to surround the city. The downtown area, where
some of the fiercest fighting had taken place, was
being rebuilt. Yet there remained, throughout the
city, large pockets of bullet-ridden and bombed out
buildings, a grim reminder of the senseless violence,
brutality and destruction that had ravaged the entire
area. Obviously I had not realized just how distressing
re-entry would be, although in reality how could it
have been otherwise? The sheer magnitude of the
war, undoubtedly one of the bitterest civil wars in
modern Arab history, was astounding. It had raged on
for nearly two decades leaving 170,000 people dead,
twice as many wounded or disabled, and approximately
two-thirds of the population dislocated. Sadly on the
political front the country was now more fragmented
and volatile than ever before. Below the surface

lurked seething hostility that stemmed from the fact that none of the major issues had been adequately addressed, nor were they likely to be in the near future.

.TWO

Upon my return two themes in particular seemed to take shape. The first centred on my academic life. For months I had looked forward to the prospect of seriously teaching again. Unfortunately I was soon overwhelmed by my responsibilities that hardly allowed time for anything else. A heavy course load, endless and highly charged meetings, long office hours, and heaps of papers to grade left me anxiously wondering how I would ever get through the day. Happily the second theme provided a much-needed respite from campus pressures. Almost instantaneously we were greeted by the gracious hospitality and warmth of old friends. Once again my husband and I stepped into a highly cosmopolitan way of life that brought together people of diverse interests and backgrounds. Our renewed encounters were enticing. I felt enormously enriched by my country's centuries-old culture.

My desire to return to Lebanon had been strong, but I seemed unable to draw strength from it. Instead a mood of dread hovered over me. I was gripped by a strange feeling of entering a world that is at once threatening and seductive. Desperately I searched for the charms and enchantments of the city, for its flavour, culture and mixture of civilizations. Then little by little, I began to isolate myself, to withdraw from all the ensuing confusion and focus my energies on work and writing. Sadly this strategy was all too reminiscent of the ugly war years when isolation became a defence mechanism against the grotesque scenes of escalating violence. The challenge ahead now seemed daunting as I groped for meaning in a realm where memory had taken the place of reality. With time, I managed to focus on the simpler joys of life. It was sheer delight to take brisk walks on the Corniche in the twilight, to gaze at the flaming sun disappear into the glittering Mediterranean Sea. The choices and rhythms of my life had changed, but deep down I was convinced that creative possibilities abound in a country like Lebanon. Throughout the centuries it has remained a place to which travellers can return, undoubtedly due to its vibrancy and cultural richness.

Finally, I decided to write historical fiction, and I knew that my desire to spin tales again was in some inexplicable way connected to my return. I stole moments from my hectic schedule to shape thoughts, craft stories and polish prose. As my cast of characters came to life, it became obvious that the female pro-tagonists shared similar attributes. Their *suspended betweenness* was a position that places them midway, as it were, between cultures. In unconventional ways it had equipped them with the fluidity necessary to merge multiple identities, and transcend the artificial boundaries of society and nationality. Undoubtedly such experiences are of immense value to those of us whose lives have been lived between worlds, who have welcomed the enriching texture of multiplicity, yet suffered its inevitable torments and confusions. My life, like the lives of my heroines, had been subjected to discontinuities and dislocations, to shifts and disruptions, to roles that must be invented again and again. Writing historical fiction, at least for the moment, satisfied my need to explore the creative potential of marginal lives. Suddenly it felt right to refocus and redefine my commitments and sense of self. Temporarily these stories offered a meaningful escape into a realm rich with possibilities.

As winter gave way to spring, a neatly typed manuscript replaced the pile of hand-written papers on my desk and my narratives assumed personal significance. No longer did I feel distracted, disillusioned, doomed. Then, as it happened, I thought of how thrilling it would be to offer a creative writing course, how refreshingly direct and of immediate relevance to the lives of numerous students. At first my colleagues in the English Department at the American University of Beirut were reluctant; after all creative writing did not fit into the traditional scheme of things. Besides, they doubted whether students would show any interest. Finally, after much deliberation, it was agreed that I should give it a try.

Within a few hours of registration, the course was completely filled. The eager students who filed into my office were impressive, and contrary to all expectations they came from a variety of disciplines. One political science major asked if I would read a forty-page play she had completed over the summer. A history student explained that she was halfway through her second short story; and an aspiring medical student wanted my comments on a collection of poems he had been working on for some time. The following semester witnessed an even sharper increase in demand. And so, additional sections were offered to accommodate the growing number of receptive students.

Initially, I was startled by how many of my students had a profound need to express themselves in their texts. Even more curious was the realization that despite their diverse disciplines, ages and backgrounds, they had a great deal in common. As the semester progressed, it became clear that fate and circumstance had conspired to transform them into seasoned travellers, border crossers, outsiders existing in the margins of whatever society they happen to find themselves in. Living between two or more worlds simultaneously, without actually belonging to any one place in particular, was a fact of life for these young people. 'Because I have never lived in any one place for very long,' wrote Yasmine, 'I don't feel I belong anywhere. I also know that I never will belong to any one place.' Ussama expressed similar feelings. 'I guess I'll end up where I've always felt most comfortable, at that point in a large circle where everyone is in the circle but I'm on the circumference watching, rarely joining in the inner circle, just watching.'

Almost immediately their stories began to echo similar themes. In no time at all, the manuscripts they had been working on were presented for response and critique, and suddenly my academic world took on new meaning. The creative energy was infectious. Workshopping texts and sharing ideas instigated an ongoing conversation that magically transformed our class encounters into charged happenings.

.THREE

I vividly recall a gripping class discussion that took place one rainy afternoon. Ali said he was having difficulty finding adequate language to describe everything that goes on in his head in his auto-biographical narrative. For some reason he sensed that whatever wording he used fell short of conveying the intensity of his feelings. What seemed to disturb him the most, is the feeling of being a complete stranger in his own country. 'Life in Canada,' he explained, 'had proceeded normally without any major upheavals. It was not my country so it was normal not to fit in. Being an outsider did not bother me.' Now the situation is entirely different. His returnee status sets him apart from mainstream Lebanese society. He feels that he is viewed with suspicion, and as he does not particularly adhere to social convention, he is perceived as being 'different from the rest', especially by an extended family that he cannot identify with, and that prides itself in maintaining 'solidarity' or 'a unified front'. If Ali is 'absorbed in a book' or 'engrossed in writing', they become immediately agitated, fearing it might contain damaging or inappropriate ideas that he could use to 'disgrace the family'. With time, Ali has become a 'tempting target' even to well-meaning relatives who are concerned that he might make them vulnerable to social criticism within the community.

Curiously as the discussion developed, students began to sound like comrades-in-arms, resorting to the use of military terms to conjure up a silent struggle. They talked about 'winning' or 'losing' the 'battle' against suspicious and distrustful social moralists who increasingly 'enforce' correct ways of behavior, who are completely convinced they have all the right answers. Consequently they 'interrogate' and 'enforce' their ways and values. Each one of them avows to speak for the family by calling on the 'reinforcement' of moral judgements to preserve the respectability of the family name. I had, by now, become so fascinated by the animated discussion, that I began to write down what students were saying.

Sana: If only they could get beyond the debunking and listen to what we have to say.
Tariq: You must be joking. They don't give a fig for our views and feelings. Besides, I find them insulting. Usually they say, "Where were you during the war?"
Sana: Exactly, I'm made to feel guilty for spending time in Europe when it was insane to remain here. They want to punish us for not being in the danger they were in.

A mixture of amused and nervous chuckles of agreement went round the room at this astonishingly frank dialogue. I listened fascinated as students expressed sentiments that had disturbed me for so long, sentiments I had been reluctant to translate into words or writing. Clearly they had no qualms about voicing their feelings on this matter. Remembering my role as an instructor, I attempted to ease the tension by summarizing their concerns. Extended family members, I suggested, seem to be fixated on looking outward instead of inward in order to eliminate the possibility of self-examination and tolerance. Instead, they narrow the focus to exclude rather than include human diversity, thus preventing people from living together in mutual respect and recognition. Generally such behaviour seems to stem from the fear of nasty gossip, what people might say, or how they might ostracize a particular family if one of its members appears to be different or strange. I was reminded of a quote I had jotted down in my journal a week before. It had to do with exiles returning to their country of origin. 'Going into exile,' Bauman writes, 'has been recorded as their original sin, in the light of which all that the sinners may later do may be taken down and used as evidence of their rule-breaking'. (Bauman, Z., *Liquid Modernity,* Malden: Blackwell, 2002)

The buzz of conversation brought me back to reality. Our classroom was a hive of lively discussion with students all wanting to express their points of view. Rarely had I witnessed such a level of involvement and intellectual excitement among this particular group. Yet today, troubled and questioning, they were alive to ideas concerning identity and belonging in ways that reflected an unusually high degree of concern and intensity. There was an urgent need to identify with non-mainstream, forward-looking individuals who touchingly believe that they can give new shape and meaning to the society they live in. I paid attention.

We represent a silent invasion, but in reality we are the wake-up call that needs to be heeded before it's too late. (Nabil)

Students were quick to reject the romantic and nostalgic views fed to them by their parents while still abroad, dismissing these stories as wishful imaginings of homesick exiles whose emotional needs are satisfied by clinging to a vanished past. Nesrine laments the desire of her parents to reconnect at the expense of ignoring the tragic reality of a country torn apart by factional strife. 'There is a part of me that accepts the need of my parents to reconstruct a perfect past, however, I wish they would stop living in denial and see how the war has destroyed Lebanon.'

Disappointment aside, many students were perceptive enough to know that the fantasies parents instil in their children are to some degree necessary. Still the different viewpoints continue to instigate ill feelings between students and parents alike. More of a problem, inevitably, is the understandable unwillingness of students to deny or escape reality by embracing the protective measures parents wrap around themselves.

That evening as I sat on my balcony mulling over the frustration and disappointment felt by students, my gaze settled on a string of tiny fishing boats as they fanned out to dot the shimmering water with their lights. Overhead a perfectly round moon hung low in the sky like a large silver coin. Just for a moment it crossed my mind how unreal and absolutely enchanting nature can be in this tiny country. Certainly this is the stuff that captivating places are made of. Besides, it is absolutely essential on occasion to escape the ugly contradictions of one's society in order to cope with the taxing demands of daily life. Suddenly I was reminded of an episode that took place during the summer of 1992 when, taking advantage of an extended cease-fire in Lebanon, we returned from abroad for a brief visit.

Prior to our visit, our son Ramzi, who is blessed with a playful and rich imagination, became so completely captivated by the breathtaking posters of Lebanon's scenic landscapes that he immediately conjured up a secret fantasy world. So eager was he to explore the hidden mysteries of the city on our first day back, that he convinced his father to take him on an early morning stroll through the busy streets. At first, he skipped adventurously ahead of his father totally oblivious to the ravaged buildings until, little by little, reality slowly seeped in and stealthily exchanged places with his dream world. Soon he was paralyzed with fear at the sight of crumbling structures, chaos and noise. Ramzi now clung tightly to his father's hand. It was indeed a rude awakening to discover that Beirut was far from the beautiful spot he had imagined it to be.

Always a resourceful child, Ramzi was quick to devise his survival strategy. To begin with, he refused to leave the flat. Ingeniously he converted our living room into a make-believe stage where all day long he performed his favourite Broadway musicals. He kept his belongings safely tucked away in his little backpack just in case we had to escape in a hurry. The ugliness he witnessed outside was expertly blocked out of his imaginatively created space. During the war years, when Ramzi was still a toddler, he would crawl under our dining-table when severe episodes of shelling fiercely rocked our flat and inquire, in a petrified voice, whether the booms were thunder with or without water. Now, however, Ramzi was not asking questions. He knew the answers all too well and had opted to withdraw just like my students who sought alternative venues in their writing; while their parents clung to nostalgically romanticized visions of what Lebanon used to be.

Clearly writing offered students a kind of freedom from the external constraints of a threatening society in the same way that denial rendered life infinitely less painful for their parents. Writing opened up spaces for students to fill with their own vision, which necessitates a move forward devoid of the sentimental baggage and strictures that arise from unrealistic notions of the past.

Thoughts of my heroines immediately came to mind. As early as 1830 they had distanced themselves from stifling conventions in search of fresh and bold alternatives. All were future oriented, anti-tradition and richly imaginative. They too were out of place exiles, living and writing from the margins, experiencing *suspended betweenness* with all its pleasures, pains and anxieties.

.FOUR

The late-afternoon drizzle casts a silver-grey light on our classroom. Students have been frantically engaged in their autobiographical narratives for weeks, and understandably, we speak of little else. Each is consumed in the dramas and fantasies of who and what they are. Today, all have fallen under the spell of their stories, and yet, a certain tension hangs in the air. There is a compulsion to share the numerous interruptions that have characterized their young lives. We play a game in which students describe the various identities they have acquired over the past few years. They are acutely aware that having to adjust to different places and ways of life, of not actually belonging to any particular place is problematic. Juggling multiple identities, an inevitable part of the diaspora experience, means constantly losing and reinventing the self. Along with this comes isolation and confusion.

I encompass a spectrum of personalities because my life has been interrupted so many times. I have never enjoyed continuity. My existence is choppy and disconnected. (Maha)

Loss and reinvention was the mechanism to cope with separateness yet there would never be any real or lasting feelings of belonging. Students are positioned on the crossroads between cultures. All kinds of multiple identities suddenly crowd our seminar room. Marginality is a condition taken for granted, but sadly there seems to be so much pain at the centre of this kind of human experience. Often their honesty is disarming.

I have been given a life rich with experiences but also filled with confusion and hardship. However, I need to keep moving, to keep going to different places. Otherwise I will suffocate (Karim).

Ironically, students have no desire to alter their *suspended betweenness*. In fact, in some inexplicable way, they welcome being kept off balance, presumably because it necessitates the constant and creative energy that accompanies reinvention of self. Increasingly, they grow accustomed to this condition of fluidity.

Once class is over, my thoughts send me scurrying down the deserted corridor, out the campus gate and into the narrow winding streets of the city. Amidst the bustle of my favourite market, surrounded by a profusion of enticingly displayed fruits and vegetables, I wait patiently as the ingredients of our evening meal are weighed on lopsided brass scales. Here there is everything to attract the eye and delight in. Back in the welcoming quiet of our flat I start cooking to calm my dizzying ideas. The personal narratives students share in class give me the feeling that we are working side by side, combining the materials of our lives in order to shape something new. Together we chart different territory by relocating the personal in a way that allows for a more critical engagement with experiences that matter.

.FIVE

Students saw merit in the ability to remain detached; sustaining a high degree of emotional distance was viewed as an asset. The idea was not to shut out the rest of the world, but to observe from a safe distance. To achieve this, they place themselves in situations that are out of step with what is happening around them. Interestingly they opt to become situated observers who ultimately seek meaning from their gaze. Hence imagination becomes a crucial component especially since their particular ways of seeing carry narrative intentionality. Writing, to some extent, is a way of controlling the strangeness of the situation, but more importantly, hybridity can be utilized to create a liberating perspective.

My father taught me to be extremely open. Throughout my sixteen years in Nigeria. I had friends from all classes, religions and nationalities, but I did not identify with any one group. This was easy for me to do because my parents never forced any religious or nationalistic beliefs on me. When we moved back to Lebanon I was distressed by the political and religious conflicts. Luckily I like to be alone and witness what is happening around me. Often I prowl the streets at odd hours just to observe and I write about what I see. I don't like to be seen. In fact, I wish I could be invisible. (Wael)

For as long as I can remember my father struggled with a private and silent war that engaged conflicting loyalties and desires because it pitted his village roots against life in the US. As he grew older, the inevitable difficulty of moving from one culture to another became increasingly more demanding. The notion of a society governed primarily by work, speed and uniformity greatly troubled him. For all its problems, life in his Lebanese mountain village seemed, at least to him, more humane; it offered a set rhythm derived from continuity, tradition and sociability. In spite of this dilemma, for most of his life my father managed to hold his diverse worlds in balance by following an arrangement that divided the year equally between his two worlds.

Aboard the plane scattered fragments come to me. My head is filled with a haphazard jumble of disturbing thoughts of no particular importance to anyone but myself. My imagination dashes from one agonizing image to another as the plane climbs steeply. Gradually the city lights grow fainter and I am deep in the silence of the night. My desperation is induced by far more than jet lag. Awake out of necessity, yet almost catatonic with fatigue after twenty-six hours of travelling, my suspension between one state and another is reminiscent of my father's precarious situation. Only a few days ago his voice had sounded calm and determined over the phone. Boisterously he joked about feeling imprisoned in the US. I was not to worry, though, because he had taken a firm decision to return to Lebanon early this year, by mid February at the latest. Naturally I was immediately sworn to secrecy out of fear that my mother, who wanted to spend more time with her grandchildren, would most certainly thwart his plans. Now barely a week after his call, my father lay in a coma in some sterile, grey hospital thousands of miles away from the village where he longed to be. The tests were conclusive; he was brain-dead.

From the corner of my eye I glimpsed a tiny woman who sat clutching a large object wrapped in an exquisite piece of cloth. She was tissue-thin and leaf-like. Age had put deep wrinkles on her sun-beaten face. Her head was crowned by a mass of snowy hair tightly pulled back and twisted into a perfectly round bun. She remained frozen throughout the flight, stared straight ahead and spoke not a word. I watched as the flight attendant inquired if she would like some dinner. When no answer came, he paused impatiently for a moment to check his exasperation. Then very rudely, he reached out and snapped down her tray onto which he aggressively plunked her evening meal, which of course, she never touched. I was irritated by what I perceived to be cultural insensitivity. Could he not see the anxieties that paralyzed this tiny Hispanic whiff of a woman? All alone, on probably her first flight ever, she was understandably intimidated by the rules of a society entirely unknown to her, let alone the fear of flying. My imagination flitted between the spoken, unspoken, and visual messages of different worlds. How much easier to be a detached observer viewing life with distant bemusement! My students were bravely mapping this new territory. Mentally they had positioned themselves to gaze and absorb from a safe distance in order to guard against the trappings of emotional involvement.

I thought of my father, of how reluctant he had been to leave his village. Now, in a cruel twist of fate, he would be brought back to Lebanon for burial and yes, just as he had promised, he would return before mid February. I watched the sunset dim. Too sad and strung out to sleep, I struggled desperately to toss out a host of dark thoughts that tumbled through my mind.

Spring in Lebanon is beautiful. The campus is ablaze with flowers. From my office window a brilliant blue sea is visible behind a row of palm trees. Each passing seminar makes me all the more aware of how expansive and imaginative students are becoming. In the crafting of personal texts, they continue to break their silence by reversing the ability of society to render them invisible and voiceless. To do this with passion and dedication is evidence of how strong is their need to capture something different in the map of possible strategies, to bring new shape and meaning to their young lives. Above all, the desire to share experiences in the truthful exploration of what it essentially means to live between worlds is, in the final analysis, immensely important for individuals whose lives must constantly be re-imagined. Certainly these stories offer essential digressions from the official and encouraged biography of a country like Lebanon. Ultimately they may even hold the key to innovative, tolerant and diverse ways of living for societies that are desperately in need of viable alternatives.

Roseanne Saad Khalaf's essay 'Living between Worlds' is an excerpt from a memoir in progress.

DRAWING THE WAR

Lena Merhej

When she lived between Beirut and New York, the animator and illustrator Lena Merhej broke through her own reticence about her experiences during the Lebanese civil war and made the animated film *Drawing the War*. A stark, monochrome memoir, it combines childhood innocence with adult uncertainty. In the Middle East, most cartoons and animated movies have been imported. What is locally produced is mainly commercial, since animators and animation studios are scarce. Merhej, on her way to an illustration workshop in Bratislava, Slovakia, answered questions by email.

.DID YOU DRAW OR SKETCH THE WAR WHEN YOU WERE GROWING UP?

The only doodle about the war I recall seeing was not a political caricature or a drawing, but a small sketch that my brother did on all of our school books: Lebanese flags, soldiers with the star of David on their helmets, and rifle shots. I never drew anything that was related to war before *Drawing the War*. Even while starting the sketches for it, I felt I was violating certain codes. I felt extremely responsible towards what I was going to depict.

.WHY WAS THAT?

Most Lebanese avoid the past, the war. For a long time, I did the same. Oblivion, for most, is a sheltering method. When mentioning the war, many Lebanese refer to it as *al ahdeth* (the events). The usage of the word 'war' has been reduced in our language. The theme of it has been subdivided and ridiculed. Its experience has been normalized, and the war, for some, has ceased to exist. Being in a different social and cultural context in New York allowed me to reflect and to become critical about my own position towards the 'issue'.

.DOES *DRAWING THE WAR* COVER A PARTICULAR PERIOD?

There is no specific temporal or geographical reference in *Drawing the War*; rather it is the story of looking at war from the conditions imposed on its civilians. It is our story, as Lebanese, of walking on the residue of things past.

.WAS THE FILM DIFFICULT TO MAKE?

The piece flowed easily when I wrote it, as if it was always there in the back of my mind, but the language was missing, and the use of the word 'war' was shameful, difficult and boring. Hence, I needed to reconstruct the language of war. I did a questionnaire from which I collected words of objects, sounds and events related to war, and that was my starting point. In *Drawing the War*, sentences, images and scenes illustrated those words which, I feel, are the most significant and constructive memory of the war.

Another difficulty was targeting a younger audience with the subject of war. I had to experiment, altering the animation in either text or images, and I did this from observation, and through the Q+A of children and young people who watched earlier, different versions of the film.

.WHY DID YOU THINK YOUR EXPERIENCES COULD BE ANIMATED?

Drawing animation is a potential to diverge, and expand, morph, bend, and twist images like the memories that we recall. Also like the process of remembering, animation appears, transforms and moulds. This specific use of animation is closely related to the narrative of *Drawing the War*, as Lebanese memoir.

.AS A CHILD, WHAT DID YOU THINK ABOUT THE WAR?

I was born during the war. There was no other condition I could relate to, so like most childhood experiences, some things were clear and some were not. There was nothing much to understand, our rational faculties had to be focused on how to save water and find batteries for our flashlights.

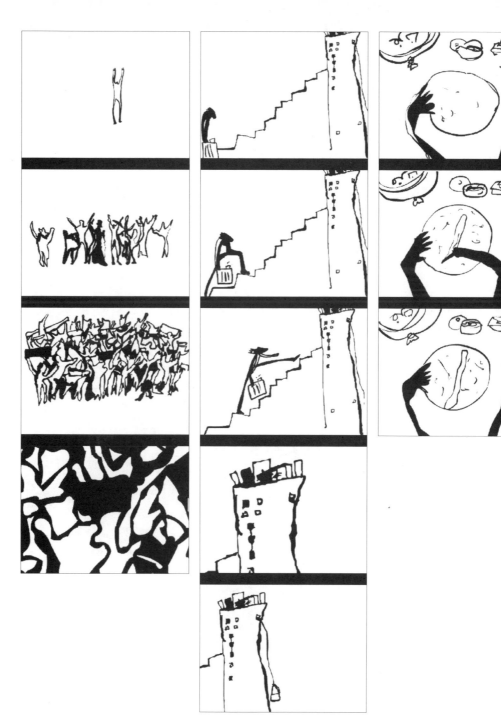

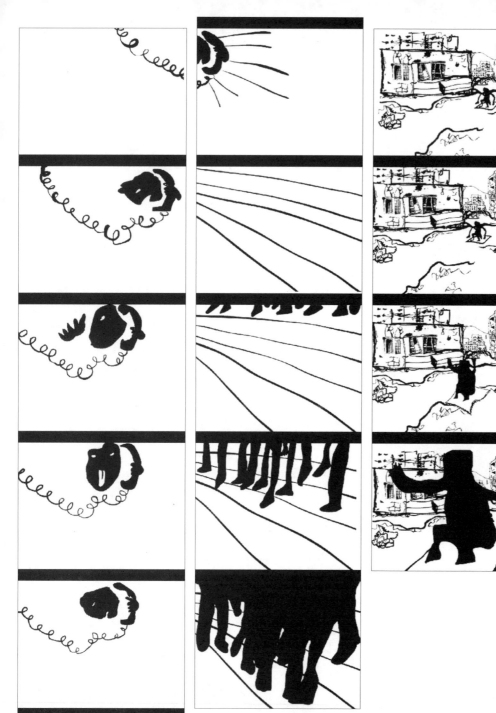

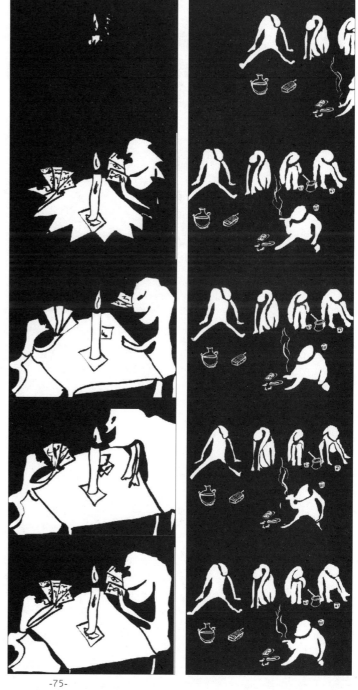

BENCHES

Omar Sabbagh

Photo by Dalia Khamissy

10 January. A piece like a segment has been cut out of the back of his head. The sun looks in and the whole world with it. It makes him nervous, it distracts him from his work, and moreover it irritates him that he should be the very one excluded from the spectacle.

Franz Kafka, *He, Aphorisms from the 1920 Diary*

If you happen to be one of the privileged inhabitants of Beirut city you might find yourself strolling through the quietly beautiful grounds of the American University on an afternoon. You might, in fact, be one of the students of this university, or perhaps one of the alumni, many of whom can be seen, with the first hints of dusk, indulging themselves in this way. Or you may be a complete outsider who, by some fortunate coincidence, has both fallen in love with these prolific vistas and is regularly mistaken for a member of staff.

If the latter, you would have probably just untangled yourself, happily and unhappily at the same time, from Hamra's cobwebby hold on you. Unhappily because Hamra's network of apathetic streets has an enchanting effect on any imagination: it crowds in on you without setting off the slightest trace of claustrophobia. The canopy of broken aerials and tipsy telephone wires overhanging the streets combined with the slouching array of shops and cafés make you feel like a weary but sated mosquito traversing the hirsute comedy of an orang-utan's body, looking for your next bite, your next inspiration. But sated, its very density can become a strain on the ear's eye and the eye's ear, so that when you emerge out of this dusty forest, into the open air of Bliss Street, something like a bird is released in your perceptual field; a giddiness.

You would have walked along Bliss, bought a *manaeesh* from Le Sage, spilled thyme all over your black duffel coat whose zipper has been panicking for three hours since it got stuck on its way up its tracks earlier that morning. You would have finished your cup of fresh orange juice bought opposite, and entered the sandy campus of the American University. If, earlier, a bird was released through your sensation as you emerged into Bliss, when you enter the American University, having been anywhere in Beirut (with all sorts of creatures released – a lion in Downtown, a panther in Achrafiye, etc), the experience is of having a bright white rabbit, counting pennies with a lisp, mounting a platypus – so patient do you become, surrounded by its multifaceted spaces for speculation and idle talk. But whether it is actually that spendthrift rabbit horny for a platypus, or whether just a squirrel giving three-quarter looks at the windowsill is a matter you decline to debate with yourself.

Directly in front of you, then, the main building appears to be a great square sulking polar bear; sulking, you assume, because it was misplaced by its creator so callously in this desert where the sand has given its fur a light beige hue, an ignominy which cannot be surpassed in polar bear lore; and sulking because the onus of a university's vertiginous administration demands seems too much of a burden for it, but it perseveres: it's known to have had a reluctant heart transplant when the campus was being renovated – it has the obsequious heart of a donkey now and has lost its aggressive aspect, happily for the students. You were not surprised to find out from one of the students that before this renovation, some students had entered this building's labyrinthine inner structure and disappeared never to return, presumably having been swallowed by its involuted, convoluted staircases, double entrances and backdoors.

You walk down the steps and through to the library. You take a left. You would now be walking along the upper part of campus that leads towards the lower half, passing on your left the three eve green benches which precede the president's mysterious residence, which have a spectacular view of the sea.

A bit in front and to your left, then, is the president's guarded home. No one is ever seen entering or exiting this building and it is rumoured that a certain gnostic sect from the last days of the Roman empire, its adepts recently reunited from the four corners of the world, meet in this residence under cover of darkness and distinction of the president's position. Whether the president himself is a member or whether just a sympathizer is unknown, and of course whether there actually is such a group is uncertain. But the rumour is enough to give this bright residence its shifty aura. It is because of this that the students turn mute when walking parallel to its walls; not a word is uttered; all conversations stop abruptly for half a minute until it is passed; they fear something, of this you are certain, but what that is, is beyond your powers of perception. If you were to continue walking, past this silent residence, a bit further on and to your right would be the legendary steps that would take you to the lower campus and onto the Corniche. These steps are notorious for being the favoured place of labour for the women staff of the American University – legend has it that to be born on these steps endows the baby boy or girl with preternatural intellectual prowess. Anyway ...

You did not go that far. In fact, you're standing parallel to the three eve green benches with one foot perched on one of the stone blocks lining the edge of the path where it drops into the sloping, heteroclite gardens separating upper and lower campus. Had you been there yesterday at exactly five-thirty, you would have witnessed, if you had concentrated, a most moving event.

It is probably best to note here that this is mid-October and at five-thirty the light is just beginning to tinge in Beirut, but that on this day, due to the heavy rain a few hours earlier, the light gave out a fresh, piercing effect, colouring the sea an intense Olympic blue. But you would have not only noticed the colour but also the roughness of the sea, which looked like a massive unmade bed, perhaps one on which a heated argument between two young lovers had just taken place. But that impression is of course only a suggestion, and if you had been there yesterday you might have put it differently.

On the third bench, then — walking from the library — you would have noticed an old lady — not very old but just beyond middle age. She has greying chestnut hair and mirthful chestnut eyes, which, no doubt, would have first attracted your attention, being so glaringly out of tune with her age. She might well be called a lady because her aura is distinctly dignified. In fact, if you were to hazard a guess, you might take her for a descendant of some Russian aristocratic family, one whose members fled south at the time of the revolution and eventually made his or her way to the Middle East, Lebanon in particular because of its cosmopolitan air. What doesn't surprise you is the majestic way she pours a beer from a bottle in a brown paper bag into a glass, tilting it straight at the last to give the drink a little extravagant head. You notice her apparel as fitting with her quiet but passionate nature. She is wearing a tan linen dress with matching shoes, and a light pewter cardigan. You also see an open book pressed face down on her left. Naturally, you assume she is taking a break from reading, having a pleasant drink in the calm surroundings. At this time there are far fewer students on campus than earlier on and, if not silence, then something approaching it settles over the campus. This is no doubt why she decides to sip her beer now, when there is no one to disturb her enjoyment of it, its scintillating fizz and coolness. And then, directly after her second inspiration of the beverage, you hear a quite extraordinary burp emitted from her lips. She sighs wearily. This is when her powerful, yet subtle declamation began.

'Of course it is much sexier, in the way I suppose Hollywood movies are sexy, to have an overpowering relation to your own self. What I mean to say is that when one has a strong inner world it tends to display itself in dramatic outward behaviour, which people might, quite naturally, find appealing. This sort of personality implies difference, dissonance with mundane reality, excitement and dare I say it romance. But is this really a healthy phenomenon? The answer to this question, however tentative, comprises, precisely, the fundament of my research. And without further introduction I will state my thesis.'

At this point she takes a quick swig of her beer and wipes the residue left on her upper lip with the sleeve of her right arm.

'It is as follows. In fact it is only what painful experience teaches, and is, in my opinion, the very nub of maturity. So. We start as fondled, adored, fussed over infants. Of course this cannot be blamed on the parents, it is only natural that such fragile creatures should be so protected. In fact, let me make it clear at this point that I do not in any way believe the parents to be at fault. They have no responsibility whatsoever. It has long been known, since Aristotle himself, that responsibility requires a free choice of alternative ways to act. A *free* choice, ladies and gentlemen. Barring extreme and unrepresentative circumstances, parents have no such freedom. It can safely be said that a balanced parent will be compelled emotionally if not socially to care for his or her young.

'So, to return to my thesis, we start blessed in this privileged state, a state wholly dissimilar from the unfortunate and grim reality of adult life. And our egos are continually fed, especially if we happen to be the youngest child of an affluent, large and loving family, which can indulge our every need and wish. This, then, is how that strong relation to self is built up in childhood. This may seem a rather banal point to you all but I assure you that merely stating such a truth and discovering it are completely different things.

'To continue to the second part of my thesis: it is only experience in the real, lonely, predatory world that begins, with each year, to distance the I from the me, making us not more selfless perhaps, but surely less self-centred. It is this transition, ladies and gentlemen, which I believe picks out the process of maturing.'

She now takes a long, slow sip of beer, puts it gently down to her right and stands up, looks directly in front of her seemingly at the sea, with a gracious, appreciative smile. It is only as she curtsies that you understand the immense importance of what has just been said. She resumes her seat and you notice a beige butterfly flutter across your vision of her. For some reason the image of this butterfly eating cornflakes voraciously shoots through your mind and with it the worry comes that there'll be none left. But this image and worry leave just as easily as they entered through one of the many dark, digressive alleys in your mind. Instantly the impact of what has just been said reasserts itself.

Had you been there yesterday you would quite naturally be close to tears by this point. You would feel the inclination perhaps to go up and shake her hand, and say a few words in appreciation. But you don't because you don't know what to say without making a fool of yourself. Of course, if you were to go up and say something, it would have to be something in keeping with the tone of the afternoon, something subtle but meaningful, something she might enjoy hearing from a complete stranger. But that's precisely it. Even if you could think of the right words to say, you are just that, a complete stranger. She might take your going up to her as a flagrant intrusion of her privacy and, even, a disruption to her peace of mind, which only too evidently is of the greatest importance. You might decide to wait and see if the right words come to you, and then, and only then, wait to see if an appropriate opportunity arises. But just as you come to this decision, a young man in light blue jeans, khaki shirt, and elegant but understated brown suede shoes – which, however, are rather worn and have an oily sheen now like sealskin – walks up to her bench and sits to the left of the down-faced book. There is something of the eagle in his features. Yes, the eagle bred with the cat. He looks briefly at her face, then at her clothes, finishing with an inspection of her shoes, and then spends a cool half-minute staring at the cover of the book lying between them. Having satisfied himself that everything is as it should be, he looks out at the sea. Perhaps he sees an unmade bed, but more likely he holds a deep belief that the great souls of the great thinkers and artists of world history reside in the sea, infusing its currents with their obvious passion, and ensuring that they are always at cross purposes, leading to the glorious wet arousals exploding near the beach. This particular way of putting it, 'glorious wet arousals', gives him great pleasure every time it occurs to him. He turns and speaks to our lady of Russian descent.

'Now I realize that I'm only a young man, but even I can see the sense and, yes, beauty in what you have just said. I don't think the parents can be blamed either. In fact I think if anything they should be con-gratulated on making the most of a very delicate situation. The father, in particular, must be applauded, perhaps even awarded, it being more natural for the mother. Yes, it was surely implied in what you said that the tenderness of the father was beyond reproach.'

Without looking at this obviously precocious young man, Anna stands up and disposes of her beer, placing the empty glass on top of the bin. She returns to her seat, picks up the book, marks the page she's on by folding its corner, closes it, and lovingly retires it on her lap.

'The father is an example to us all. He must be. Do you think the recovery would have been as swift or as relatively painless as it was if it wasn't for the father. No, of course not. I never said the father was to blame at all. Quite the contrary. But naturally the mother in a case like this has an important if often passed over role to play. Indeed, you might call it a negative role, her achievement being the very lack of action. Naturally, this is due to her heightened role at the beginning, when that overpowering relation to self was being built up. You will remember in particular the way she would sleep with him in his bed for five minutes each night until he was six years old. How was it he requested? "Will you sleep with me three times?" putting up three fingers, not yet knowing his numbers well yet, or even aware of the word "minute". And she would give him that comfort each night. Of course she can't be to blame, no matter how different the world out there is to the warmth of that comforting ritual each night.'

A small group of girls now pass the two interlocutors, and the young man, whose name is Nadim, is distracted momentarily by one of the pert bottoms, packed in grey denim, gently swaying before him.

'You think he *has* recovered then?' he said, his composure cracking slightly for the first time.

'On the whole, yes.' With this Anna's face, which up until now had given off an air of graceful, scholarly detachment, sweetened instantaneously, and her smile was so wide it threatened to tear her face apart. The word 'clownish' entered Nadim's head, faced with this smile. But then it eased a little, and her slightly teary eyes met his for a brief moment; she reached over and touched his left cheek with her right palm, held it there momentarily and then pulled it away slowly.

'You're thinking about the nightmare he had when he was nine years old, aren't you?' speaking with tenderness now.

'Yes. It was here, in this city, during one of his summer holidays. But if he's recovered as you say, I don't see how it can be of any importance now.'

'I think you'd be surprised. A vision like that in retrospect might be viewed as a premonition of some magnitude. Black and white warring in motion, fading into each other where they meet in the middle without creating any grey, it might be explained as the whiff of a latent psychic division. No, I think you're right to bring up the nightmare. It's true, on the whole he has recovered, but the nightmare, coming as it did so far in front of any serious problems, might help him in dealing with the residual symptoms now.'

Nadim now noticed her small brown handbag for the first time as she extracted a biscuit from it, one he recognized to be a custard cream. As she took her first bite, crumbs sprayed from her lips all over the front of her dress, but Anna seemed oblivious, deep in thought as she was, toying with the idea of that nightmare and the possible insights its recent discovery might contribute to the case in hand. He thought her a magnificent woman, and was grateful not only for the appropriate choice of biscuit, but for the effort she was evidently making.

Had you been there yesterday you would have noticed by now how the flies, which normally torment those seated at the place in question, were curiously absent. The army of kittens, some cream-coloured, some thyme coloured, some of whom it would not be farfetched to call purple, abstained from its usual polyphonic scream of hunger. Indeed, you would have perhaps been shocked by the almost conspiratorial respect the surroundings effected, the gentle breeze being most conspicuous.

Doubtless, then, the gentle breeze would not have gone unnoticed. And neither would the kittens. In fact one of them, a starving striped kitten, started to make what it no doubt thought to be sympathetic noises: 'Oowww … oowww'. You assumed it was attempting to anglicize the Arabic cry of pain: 'aiyy' to the Anglo-Saxon 'ow'. Or, that it was trying to imitate the much-loved dog. You could not tell which. It jumped onto the bin, pinning its claws on the lower edge of the gap where refuse is thrown and slowly dragged itself up, curling its head and neck into the bin in its scrounge for food. Anna stopped to watch the spectacle, amused; Nadim looked on, angrily, because it reminded him of a joke an American acquaintance of his had made a few months earlier. Nadim was staring at a cat, which had just given birth to its litter under one of the many staircases of the university. The cat had hissed aggressively at him. This dangling American had obviously been watching: he came up to Nadim, introduced himself, and said: 'You may be thinking that it's trying to ward you off, being protective of its young. Hah! You're in Lebanon my friend. Don't you know that it's perfectly normal for a mother to entice young, eligible men in this way as prospective suitors for her daughters.' He then burst into a raucous laughter. Nadim had winced, looked away and walked off in a different direction.

But, no; perhaps it was not Anna's mirthful chestnut eyes that first attracted your attention when you happened to be passing those three eve green benches, which precede the president's mysterious residence, positioned at the hilt of a promontory overlooking the sea, and protected by evergreens, noble sentries standing behind and between. In fact it seems more logical that you would have been first accosted by the sight of a plump thirty-something-year-old man sitting, smoking an elaborately made hookah, which is clearly his own property brought specially for the occasion – there being no waiting service at these benches – sitting rather languidly, legs crossed, on the first bench. Not only does it seem more logical, the first coming before the third, but also more likely, his dishevelled appearance being more striking, as well as the peculiar nature of his thoughts at this time.

The lines of his face best resemble those of a bulldog, and are made fuzzy by the fact that it hasn't shaved for at least a week. His hair is not so much long as unbrushed, but not completely chaotic. He wears glasses, small black circular glasses (perhaps it was this simple fact alone that attracted your attention) and a bright, plain tangerine T-shirt above baggy light grey suit trousers with turn-ups. His shoes you do not notice so there is little point in mentioning them here. With his left hand he is smoking an emerald green hookah with silver-plated pipe, and with his right he occasionally scratches his right thigh or behind his right ear. When he commits this latter action, he sucks at the hookah with more determination, curling his lips in towards his mouth as he does so. It seems a reasonable thing to do so you concentrate more on his gaze, which, expectedly, is transfixed by the sea below, his eyes bulging behind the lenses emptily. But fortunately you are able to follow his thoughts quite accurately so you are not worried by such apparent emptiness, which might fool someone less attentive.

Why this is the case you cannot quite work out, but when he looks at the sea he thinks neither of an unmade bed nor of great souls buried therein, but rather of a massive hall full of tipsy cocktail waitresses in short skirts chattering incessantly and milling about in such numbers that they seem animal-like. But this image is of less importance than the sound of the loudspeaker in the background booming out the voice of his doctor, whom he visited earlier that day for the results of his routine check-up. The voice nonchalantly announces that he has lung cancer. Why you hear this voice in his head in a nonchalant tone is due more to this youngish man's current mood, than to the actual tone of the doctor earlier that day. That doctor's voice was certainly not nonchalant, but rather highly animated due to the gravity of the news and even more so due to the surprising correlation of the results and the patient's age. It is, as you no doubt already know, much rarer to have cancer of the lungs at this relatively young age. His mood, then, is not very excited but seems, at least this is how you interpret it, indifferent, indifferent but pensive. Let us get this clear, he is most definitely thinking about the situation, but what is so interesting about this scene, gripping even, is the attitude of his ruminations. You might have even smiled when you wryly chose the word 'angle' (of his thoughts) over 'attitude', at the time.

'I see, and how long do I have to live, assuming I do not take treatment,' he had asked.

'I would say between six and eight months,' the doctor replied.

'Will it be excessively painful?'

'Only towards the end.'

Only towards the end. He thinks he'll cross that bridge when he comes to it, because that is the only bridge that needs crossing. The naked fact of his death, the 'cashing in of his mortality' as it were (a phrase he has since devised), does not seem to upset him unduly. This attitude, or 'angle' as you will have it, is very clear in his mind, and repeatedly crystallizes with each exhalation of smoke. The girls' bottoms that pass him by do not distract him from these thoughts, and you find it an effort to keep up with the intensity of his thinking without getting side-tracked yourself. But to get back to his attitude, it is precisely the clarity of this attitude that upsets him. If he has been in any way inconvenienced by this morning's news it is only by the realization it has forced upon him – that he never made it back to life after he recovered all those years ago, but hid away in the academy, in some place between real living and death. He comes to the conclusion that he has rested comfortable in this non-life of learning, away from the highs and lows of a life made vulnerable to the impact, yes, impact is the exact word he is looking for, of other human beings. It is this form of infantile hiding since his recovery, which he seems to have forgotten about and mistaken for real life all this time, that makes the prospect of death not exactly appealing, far from it, but just un-frightening, neutral.

Had you been there yesterday at five-thirty exactly, on seeing this uncomely, youngish man thinking these unpleasant thoughts, you might have found it more upsetting than gripping, and moved on to the spectacle of the third bench, skipping the second. Indeed, perhaps that is what you did do.

As far as you are concerned you may well have done that. But merely having the intention of doing something, however powerfully willed, cannot be equated with the actual doing of it. On your way to the third bench (and once again the stern grimace of logic might easily be invoked), where that most moving event awaits you, you could not but notice the scene presented to you on the second bench. You are well aware that Islamic fundamentalism is at a high at this period of world history, but this knowledge never prepared you for the sight of a full-but-trim-bearded mullah standing behind this bench, regally robed, massaging the shoulders of a somewhat younger, rather scruffily-bearded man, who is clearly his student. This mullah grips his student between thumb and index finger, pressing rhythmically as he makes a noise like a young child pretending to fly an airplane. All the while the younger man, the massagee, nasally chants the Muslim prayer call, one moment sorrowfully and the next in a gay sing-songy way, switching back and forth between the two, and occasionally being completely drowned out by the 'nniiyyaaoowww' of his mentor.

Had you been there yesterday at this time you would have marvelled at the idiosyncratic manner in which these two gentlemen viewed the sea. The first saw millions, perhaps billions, of tattooed hands waving all the world's national flags simultaneously. The second did not. What exactly he saw was so scandalous that you would not have it mentioned here. You are to be commended on your taste. And when the group of girls with pert bottoms packed tightly in denim passes, both men affect indifference and do not flinch. However, you are genuinely amused by the large erection that has just emerged beneath the cream robe of the younger, seated gentleman. He does not react in the hope that it will pass unnoticed; naturally, you feign ignorance being a kind-hearted soul. Once again, you are to be commended for this behaviour.

But you were probably just about to lose your cool at this point when you suddenly, and fortunately – you definitely felt that this impulse to move was fortuitous at the time – moved on to the spectacle presented by the third bench.

You now see Anna munching away at a custard cream with a brooding brow that betrays her deep concentration – no doubt to do with some esoteric or at least scholarly topic – and Nadim sitting sideways to her left with his right leg folded across the bench, his right elbow hinged against it propping up his head, watching her intently with the overt air of someone awestruck. For some reason you see all this, and only this (nature retaining its brilliant colour) in black and white. If you are honest this does not annoy you half as much as might have been expected given the preferences you have shown in much of your recent photography.

Nadim is thinking, with a grotesquely concentrated facial posture engraving the dimples in his cheeks, 'I wonder if she has a boyfriend? I could ask her out but she might reject the offer. Safer to keep it like this and then later, later we'll see.' He picks at the invisible spaces separating his teeth with his left thumbnail, and then speaks.

'I think he loved her in his own way. I don't think it would be too far-fetched for someone to say he genuinely loved her, do you? Even if you take into account the lack of real dialogue, when it comes to the validity of an emotion I can't believe you'd insist on defining "reality" as the physical universe. Or, if what you are trying to tell me is that what *she* was thinking all the while might possibly contribute to any conclusion about whether and to what extent he loved her, then I'm afraid, with respect, I will have to disagree. As far as I'm concerned he loved her. What is it they say? The feeling is merely a chemical process equivalent to certain, manageable, quantities of dark chocolate. A chemical process! Well surely if that is the case, and I realize I'm only a young man to be saying this, then he was in love with her. Yes, admittedly "in love", I grant you that simply "love" was too strong a verb.'

'But that *is* a physical explanation,' Anna blurts out, looking up ponderously from her breast, upon which her head had nestled for the past minute or so. 'But I agree, how she felt is immaterial, indeed *she is*, to all intents and purposes, immaterial. But I don't think he was even *in* love with her. I think it was much more complicated than that. I'm afraid it comes down to the effect that canine teeth crooked to a certain extent, on both sides of a mouth that smiles goofily, on a face that has yellow-ochre curls bouncing about its sides, has been known to have on young men of his age. As I said it is a physical explanation. It can be irrevocable, but in this case it seems he has recovered sufficiently.'

Anna now retrieves another icy beer bottle from inside her handbag. She cracks it open with her teeth – you cringe because you tried this once in your teens and broke one of your teeth – and takes a swig from it directly. Had you been there yesterday at five-thirty exactly you might have thought this a vulgar way to behave, unbecoming of so evidently elegant a mind. But before you can get worked up about this matter another group of girls pass you. You are compelled to follow the ebb and flow of a dull, dark turquoise bottom belonging to one of these girls. You follow it past the point where the steps to lower campus begin. You assume they are taking the long route to that other arcadia, the oval, passing on their way the fuchsias, lilacs, violets, periwinkles, yellows, browns, greens, of the university's lovely layered gardens; there, the benches are serenaded by palm trees. And just as you are picturing what to you has always seemed the obscenity of palm trees you remember Anna and Nadim. When you return your gaze to the third bench you find the young man is no longer there and Anna is calmly sipping her beer from the glass now, which is no longer on top of the bin.

LET'S SPEND THE EVENING IN THAT NEW RESTAURANT – AFTER ALL, IT'S THE MOST AMERICAN

Hasan Daoud

The Henry J. Beenes Restaurant – called 'Hank's' by its friends – is the latest craze in restaurants. In fact, in the successive waves of eating establishments that Beirut has seen, it's the newest one to be imported from abroad. These restaurants compete in an ongoing race, the new ones wiping out the old or suddenly appearing. Hank's, located in Quraytam, is the latest contender. Everything in it is American, from the crossing of the threshold to the end of the meal. The building is American: its design harkens back to the nineteenth century. The colours and numerous signs are American too. So are the photographs inside, and the large metal and paper advertising banners. In fact, not only are they American but they were brought from America to be hung on the walls here. The brass beer tap is American. The waiters, triumphant supporters of the restaurant who wear its name embossed on their shirts, are local Lebanese but they serve in an American way. And they are perpetually working on improving their style: one tosses a glass bottle to another who neatly catches it after it has flown through the air. Or they sit with the customers, or by themselves at tables meant for customers. Sometimes one of them leaps across the bar for amusement or to instruct diners on the art of having fun.

At Henry J. Beenes, the young women who pour in try to be like Americans, exchanging 'hellos' in English – or in 'American' – with the hostess at the door. It doesn't trouble them to remain standing while they sip their drinks; in fact, they probably like it that way, and do it intentionally. Standing there, they start speaking in 'American' to each other even though it is their second or third language, after Arabic and French. People still consider it better to educate their children in French schools because, of course, they'll be taught English there, too. English is easy, they say, and their son or daughter will have it down perfectly after a year of study in the first year of middle school. French is difficult, so a child must begin with it while still young. Their decision is helped by the abundance of French schools in Lebanon, remnants of a bygone era. They also like to be able to say that when their child goes abroad to specialize, he or she won't need to go any further than France, which, in their way of thinking, is not so far away at all.

The children are educated in French, but they do not speak it. The language has become more or less what Latin was in European schools. French has become the language of Lebanese schools, but 'American' English is the language of everyday speech, charming ways and what's new – not only for adolescent pupils, but also for later when they encounter the trials and tribulations of adult life. French then will remain the language of the family, since none of them will use it except when speaking to relatives on the telephone, asking politely after their health.

At the international commercial fairs that are held in Beirut, English has become the language of choice, not only for exhibitors communicating with customers but also for all the fair-goers who come to show themselves off. Even the French men standing at the French booths have begun to speak to their customers in English, which they pronounce in their own particular way.

The Lebanese who carry French citizenship – and whose participation in events concerning French presidential elections broadcast on television here in Lebanon – may appear to observers as a minority with their old-fashioned way of speaking. When they gathered in front of the camera, awaiting brief remarks by the

French ambassador who would soon drink a toast with them in honour of the winner, they all looked so old. 'Oldies', in the sense that Beirutis use the word, when referring to certain restaurants that offer with the meal a spate of singing from the 1960s. In the restaurant on Rue Makhoul, the oldies singer sang twenty songs and about fifteen of them were American, even though the diners in their sixties would have preferred French songs, on the whole.

In any case, they do not attempt to keep up with their younger fellow citizens, adolescents and those just a bit older, who try to enter firms, agencies and financial institutions early. Those younger people want things to be American, and fully so. That is why restaurants catering to the young set hardly last any time at all. They fold as soon as a seemingly more authentically American restaurant arrives on the scene. As for burger joints, new ones put their predecessors out of business before falling into the clutches of the big companies. This isn't so much about the quality of the food, it's more about the restaurant's ability to disseminate an atmosphere of American-ness around the food. Not long ago, a restaurant that opened near Rue Verdun was organizing auto racing and inviting its customers to rally there and set up committees. At another restaurant, established earlier, the diners began to toast the American colonel who invented the mixture of herbs and spices for Kentucky Fried Chicken. In the case of Henry J. Beenes, its customers have begun to appear in the streets wearing T-shirts printed with the restaurant's name and catchphrase.

These restaurants boast a national dimension that necessitates the transformation of customers into partisans. 'You won't find a seat there,' the friend who went to this new restaurant before we did told us. Indeed, the large dining area was packed, and there were more people waiting. 'Even though they don't treat them well,' said the friend who observed that the waiters formed their own group and were inattentive to the customers. When we finally sat down, our entire conversation was limited to how the other diners spoke, what they were wearing and the fact that we had become old-fashioned.

UP
AND DOWN
MY NOSE

Anonymous

'Merci Oh! Merci pour ce nez qui ne m'a jamais causé de soucis.'

'Thank you, thank you for this nose that has never given me any worries,' sang Anne Sylvestre, the French *protégée* of Georges Brassens and one of the voices that enchanted my youth. I loved listening to her songs, embracing their meaning with enthusiasm, in particular her 'Thank you' line. Yes, Anne Sylvestre, the French woman with long brown hair, did not have a cute, turned up nose like other European stars, far from it. More to the point, she was proud of what she was and held her guitar with beauty and dignity. This singer/poet was reinforcing my revolt against my environment, and in particular against Rima, the girl in my classroom who kept advising us all on how to look pretty which was obviously synonymous to looking European. Rima was adamant that she was blessed with a trimmed and very turned up nose because, whenever possible, she had been incessantly pushing its tip upwards with her index finger. I can only shrink with shame when I think how ridiculous we must have looked — all twenty-five girls in the classroom — writing our essay with one hand and pushing our noses up with the other.

I do not know anything about Rima's where-abouts and if she is satisfied with her life, but I often find myself singing.

'Thank you, thank you Anne Sylvestre! You have helped me avoid Dr K, the famous Lebanese plastic surgeon and his carving knife.' His knife has been used on many women of my generation in Lebanon. My Iranian friend Ziba, who did not have her nose done, told me about Dr B, the equally famous beauty surgeon of pre-Khomeini Tehran. Ziba also wanted to be proud of who she was. 'Good or Bad! This is who we are,' we exclaimed in unison.

In Paris, meeting regularly in a coffee shop in the fifteenth *arrondissement,* the stronghold of Lebanese and Iranian refugees, Ziba and I liked to play a game. We would look around, spotting ladies with turned up noses and we would try to figure out which of the two doctors they had entrusted their noses to. Many Middle Eastern ladies sitting at neighbouring tables had astonishingly small and turned up noses, or so it seemed to our proud but somehow nasty selves. We both knew that our joke was not entirely innocent. 'Are we not a bit envious?' I dared ask her one day. 'Do we really have no regrets whatsoever about our decision to keep our Semitic and Persian smelling tools in their natural state?' After all, neither one of us was very keen on nature: we loved the city, illusions and the theatre more than we cared for trees, cows and wild virgin spaces.

The contradiction we would not fully admit to ourselves was that of plastic surgery itself. We both knew that if you let nature be without interfering with it, our species would be in deep trouble, and the world a crueller place than the one we are living in today. Nature is unjust, human interference tries, without always being successful, to make life fairer.

Newspaper advertisements for plastic surgery

Our attitude, Ziba's and mine, strikes me as being at best contradictory and politically correct in the worst sense of the word: for had we not spent many hours in our teens hiding pimples under some artificial cream that imitated the colour of our otherwise smooth skin? Had we not spent hours at the hairdresser trying to straighten our hair, and even longer hours crimpling it into a carefree Afro-style? Yes, said we. Ziba and I tried to sound rational, for we were not cutting through our skin and bones, but we were artificially beautifying ourselves. Easily said when surgical aesthetics used to cut flesh rather than pumping silicone up and down the body. No! There definitely is no rational response to the lure of plastic surgery.

I have noticed, whenever I am in Beirut or when I visit Rio de Janeiro – two cities where surgical interventions with the lips, thighs and nose are becoming so common that your next door neighbour has undoubtedly undergone plastic surgery at least once or twice – that people still say: 'Oh but she is not a natural blonde,' as if to make her blondeness less admirable. Or: 'She only looks young because of a face-lift,' meaning she is not as good as you think she is. Resorting to nature to diminish the aesthetic value of a person, a woman in particular, is not only the revenge of the poor, or those who have not dared go through the surgery of a Dr B or a Dr K, but perhaps more pernicious. We do not like to be ashamed of what we are, and going through surgery to look different, generally more beautiful, is an admission that we are not good or not good enough. This became obvious to me two months ago, when I met Chadia, who was blessed with a 'perfect' nose, but had a recent nose job to make it even cuter because: 'I want people to tell me that my nose is perfect.' It seems that we humans still believe in the superiority of nature's arbitrariness over our own creative initiative. People still admire the aristocracy, even when it is broke and pitifully useless.

But why Lebanon and Brazil? Why is plastic surgery more pervasive in these two countries than McDonald's and Pizza Hut? Is it because women are more valued there for their shape than for their achievements? Statistics don't agree with this conclusion. For as far as women's work and their role in society is concerned, they do not score less than other equivalent but less 'beautified' places. Is it because on this shore of the Mediterranean, and on that flamboyant side of the ocean, people like to exhibit themselves assertively? Are these two countries so enamoured with gloss and stardom, that the seamstress and the waitress, as well as the rich housewife, want to look as glamorous as their TV idols? Maybe, but the phenomenon is becoming international. A friend of mine who had studied medicine decided to specialise in plastic surgery. 'I want to become rich,' he explained unapologetically when I inquired about the motives for his choice. Now this rich and famous doctor tells me that even the 'austere Brits' are paying exorbitant prices to reduce the belt of fat around their hips or waist. Men are discretely but increasingly visiting his clinic. Recently a lady coming from the Middle East told him that she needed her nose done immediately. She wanted it turned up. 'It is urgent,' she said, 'I'll pay you double if you do it now.' Then he asked her why she managed to live with her nose for forty years and suddenly couldn't wait a month to have it done. 'I am the only one with a nose "like ours" left in the office!' she replied. 'Soon, she is going to be the only one without the sexy, puffed up lips,' I said to the doctor.

Of course the doctor is not afraid of running out of work. Beauty after all is purely subjective, and he has read during his years of training about the aestheticians who, for many years, tried to turn women's lips into small tiny lines, and the painters who added fat around women's bellies and waists with a few strokes of their brush.

'We shall always try to bend nature and feel guilty about it,' said my doctor friend philosophically, feeling safe about his future. And me, I shall keep on singing 'Thank you Anne Sylvestre!' But not too loudly.

THE
LONG VIEW

If not made in heaven, the romance between the camera and altitude began at the turn of the last century when cameras were first suspended from hot air balloons. Today, photogrammetry, the science of making measurements and maps from photographs, has advanced to the point that an ordinary soldier can be distinguished from a general, by the style of his shoes. This detailing has meant that much of the technology and images are classified by the military.

It is impossible to publish vertical images of Beirut without the permission of the Lebanese Army. The photographs on the following pages were taken between 1995 and 1999 from a plane belonging to MAPS Geosystems in Beirut. They are oblique views, shot from varying heights between 5,000 and 30,000 feet, which show the evolving mosaic of the city. As the quantum theorist Erwin Schrödinger has remarked, 'The task is not so much to see what no one has yet seen, but to think what nobody has yet thought, about that which everybody sees.'

Saint Georges, 1996

American University of Beirut, 1997

EL-Metn Jal-Dib, 1997

Saint Georges General Overview, 1999

Saint Georges, 1997

Beirut Central District, 1996

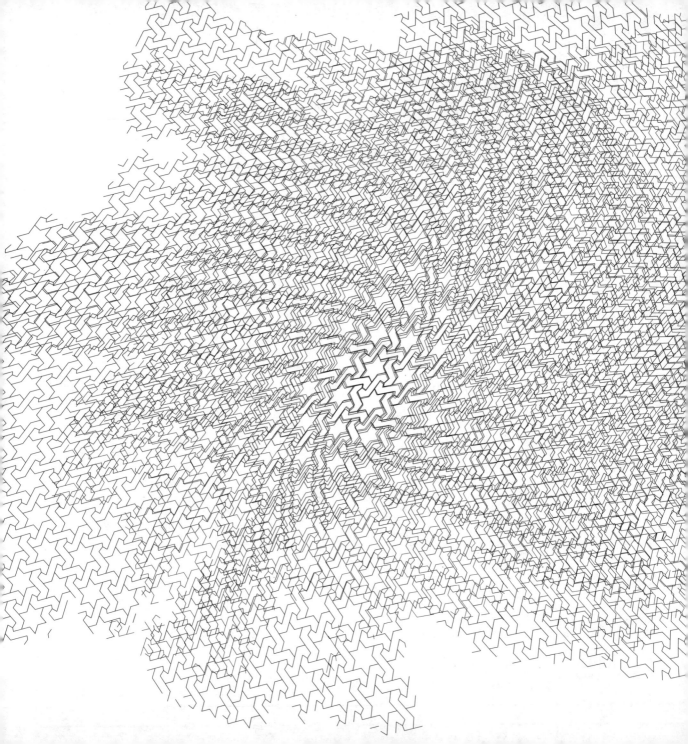

SUSPENDED

CROSSINGS: BEIRUT IN THE EIGHTIES

Hazim Saghie
Photos by Nabil Ismail

When the Israelis advanced towards Beirut, I felt puzzled. Is this normal, when the Israelis are in Khalde by the airport, only a few kilometres from where I'm living in al-Mousaitba? 'Israel' is a word familiar to me since I was a kid. I learned it as a swear-word in the same way foreigners learn a new language through its expletives. So how could I feel ambivalent when Israel had come as an invader to my country? Of course, I was afraid, especially since the explosions – the sorties of the planes, and shelling – were new to my ears. This same feeling was shared by a few Lebanese I knew and many I didn't.

I still remember how pale Hasan's face became when Nabil stood up on a chair – and Nabil was already quite tall – and extended his hands upwards, stretching as far as he could. Nabil was trying to impersonate the Israeli missiles he saw while working as a photographer in the south. He started making sounds – 'Boom!' 'Arghghgh!' – imitating the noises made by the weapons advancing towards us. Then he swore by God, the Qur'an, his mother and sisters that he was telling the truth.

Immediately Hasan insisted that his family should leave the city. He grabbed his wife Nada's hand as if they were starting their escape that very moment. But we all tried to calm him down. I told him, 'Look Hasan, you always want to escape to the south when it gets terrible in Beirut and the local militias fight. Now it's different. The danger is coming from the south. So where are you going to run?'

Of course, fear had become a familiar friend. I felt a member of a tiny sect which used to panic every time anything happened. But there was another feeling, stronger than fear, which was behind our cold neutrality, our black neutrality that could appear yellow to others. For years Beirutis had felt that they were insignificant – that no one consulted them about their lives and the total anarchy that pervaded their city. Their existence was taken for granted. And they were used to taking themselves for granted as much as the outside world did. Lebanon was called 'a playground' and their capital a strategic site. They couldn't push their noses into what had been decided by the regional players and superpowers. The resentment of my small group found some outlets in articles, essays and a few petitions, but these only brought us trouble. Some people accused us of being 'isolationists' because we wanted an exit from the war to bring back a Lebanese state once more. When Yasser Arafat paid a visit to our newspaper, *As-Safir*, my colleague Abdullah was one of the people who received him. Abdullah did not hesitate to provide the PLO leader with an eloquent description of the situation in Beirut. He told Arafat that 'if the Palestinian fighters really loved Palestine they should leave it to the Jews.'

Arafat was shocked, and he thought Abdullah was making a joke that went too far. But my colleague wasn't joking, he was very serious and he had a whole theory to back it up. The lover, if truly in love with the other person, should sacrifice everything for the other person's happiness. If another lover comes along who can provide a better life, the lover should release his loved one. So Abdullah concluded that if the Palestinian revolution didn't want Palestine to end up like war-torn Beirut, it was better to leave it to the Israelis.

The widespread wisdom then was that as long as dozens of Lebanese and Palestinian armed factions, not to mention the Syrian forces, were abusing Beirut and its inhabitants, what was the big fuss if Israel was added to the list of violators? If five or six groups were raping the city, why not seven? At that time I was extremely disturbed by how angry we were with the Israelis but not with our own 'brothers'. I wasn't aware of many things that I would come to realise later.

Yes, the Arabs abused Lebanon, but the Lebanese abused it as well. At the same time, the Arabs broke the narrowness of Lebanon's mountain mentality. They brought money as well, which the Israeli invasion dried up, totally cutting Beirut off from the outside world.

Nevertheless, the difficult circumstances that preceded 1982 deprived me of my ability to tolerate what I perceived to be irrational. I was a bundle of anger, a calculator which counted other people's stupidities. I confronted their fanaticism with a fanaticism of my own. Mine was not violent and it accumulated inside me, while my enemies found release for theirs in the street clashes. So they were much happier than me. Because I attributed this massive stupidity to the militias in West Beirut where I was living, I decided to leave my city to the invaders and those who wanted to fight them and move to East Beirut with my small family. We were among huge numbers of people who also moved eastwards.

.TWO

The crossing between al-Barbir and al-Mathaf in the summer of 1982 was crowded with cars and people who were only interested in carrying on with their lives; they didn't want to fight. Some of them wanted water, some of them were carrying babies, as if the tiny creatures were pleas for compassion and mercy since they were Muslim families going among Christians for sanctuary. At the checkpoints the 'Lebanese forces' gave us an uneven reception. They welcomed those who looked prosperous, and thoroughly searched those who didn't, especially if they were single men without families. The checkpoints were not governed by blind ideological sectarianism. They were motivated by an eclectic and organised hypocrisy that had shocked me even before my move to East Beirut. I had started going to the east side in 1980 after years of refusing to set foot in the 'isolationist' areas. I went following a personal political change which made me view both sides with the same critical gaze. In repeated weekend visits to escape militia clashes in West Beirut, I started to accept and even coexist with the place. At the beginning, I was totally repulsed by the numerous pictures of Bashir Gemayel and other evidence of the militias, like armed men in the street. Gradually however, I who had come from Pan-Arabism, Marxism and Khomeinism, started to feel that in East Beirut they had succeeded in dividing time and space between the armed and the unarmed. While in the west, there were daily, armed clashes, in the east we could go for long periods without gun battles. They

The Green Line at al-Mathaf crossing, 1988

had created a zone free of military politics where life continued almost normally. Because this was so different from West Beirut, many other people from that part of the city had started to make weekends visits to Broummana, Jounieh and Achrafiye in the east. My emotions then were like the flow and ebb in a single wave.

Still, in 1982, I felt a bit out of place in East Beirut as I watched, from Beit Meri, the Israelis destroy the west side. Not everyone in the east was equally moved. Some of them seemed genuinely sorry. Others were relieved and even appeared to be enjoying themselves. But in all cases their moods were not mine. So once again, I was part of a tiny minority, and the sect I had chosen comprised those who, like myself, had escaped. We used to derive the material for our conversations from memories of the west or from news of friends scattered all over Lebanon or abroad. I often found myself engaged in fierce arguments 'defending Muslims'

The crossing at al-Mathaf, 1988

from fanatics in the east the way I used to have violent conversations 'defending Christians' against extremists in the west.

Despite everything, the west had given me a space I didn't have in the east. You could walk a few metres and find yourself in a café or maybe by the sea. This feeling of freedom that no one could harm us, that we were surrounded by the people we knew, was enough before the kidnapping of foreigners began.

The problem with East Beirut was that it was like cities in the Gulf or the US. You had to drive endless kilometres in order to reach a café in Jounieh where more often than not you found no one to sit with. And this long drive was not friendly. The people were strangers; the landmarks and signs unfamiliar. So the best choice was to stay at home, waiting for 'visitors' from 'the Lebanese forces' to come and take me to their nearest jail. Some sought refuge from this alienation in nature and went to the mountains. But I found even more estrangement in the wilderness, which nothing could overcome. Every time I travelled north-wards from Beirut towards the mountains, thousands of cars crowded the roads. I couldn't dispel from my imagination the image of tiny mechanical creatures rushing crazily and chaotically to nowhere. Any one of these creatures might try to stamp out the others in a brutal race which led them to the valley of no return, where they would all die at the end of the road.

The eastern areas had been hastily fabricated, dictated by a military impulse which made instincts permanently mobilised behind a façade of silk and velvet. And every time one got closer to these instincts one realised that the war made the two parts of Beirut the same, though in a different way. Life continued like that until bombs were dropped on West Beirut for two consecutive days and I thought of going back to see my friends and check on my apartment, which I had loaned to a communist writer. I had given him the keys when his own house had been hit by an Israeli bomb. Out of respect, I rang my doorbell three times and when nobody answered, I opened it with my own key only to hear very strange noises coming from deep within the apartment. More curious than worried, I walked inside and discovered to my amazement that the noise was coming from the bathroom, where the writer had decided to live, surrounded by numerous plates and coffee cups. He was sitting and reading. I asked him to come out and told him there was no need to stay in there as it was safe today; the Israelis were not shelling, the evidence being that I could cross the city safely. Very hesitantly he came out, telling me that he preferred to spend most of his time sitting on the toilet because the sound of shelling was very loud and could come unexpectedly. Once he relaxed, he started telling me about the mistake his party had committed by fighting a sectarian and nationalist war when their raison d'être was class and social issues. It was as if he was confessing. Of course he knew I

was not on good terms with the Communists and I hated, especially in a moment like that, to play the role of a priest. On the other hand, the man's weakness appealed to me, although to my taste he had gone too far in declaring it. In the enclosed rooms, surrounded by the deserted city, our conversation had a unique flavour. It reminded me of Marcello Mastroianni and Sophia Loren in *A Special Day* about Hitler visiting Mussolini. But this was not the appropriate time for gloating. I told him that everyone makes mistakes and he should not be preoccupied with political mis-calculations. Then I said goodbye and returned to East Beirut. After the Israeli invasion he wrote a fiery article about the steadfastness of Beirut in which he fiercely attacked 'the opportunists and cowards' who fled east.

Today I don't feel any anger towards this man, but he makes me consider both war and ordinary life, when each of us returns to our herd. Wartime is full of fear and if it causes an individual to betray his group, the period afterwards must be filled with unlimited guilt, apology and exaggeration, even at the expense of others. We started reading long essays and poems about the heroism in Beirut, which became an overstated myth. On the other hand I saw another version of the same heroism in East Beirut after Gemayel was elected president. People fell under the spell of mass hysteria. They started to mythologise and express vengeful tendencies. The factories of amplified imagination only stopped working after Bashir's assassination. In fact, from the very beginning, I saw in his rise a tragedy not only for the ideals I believed in but also for me personally, for my friends and an entire generation. It was as if an era ended in which the names of Nasser, Lenin and Guevara, Ho Chi Minh and Mao, as well as the latecomer Khomeini, would be replaced by a new period with its own visionaries.

In Beirut, things started to unfold quickly. The death of Bashir triggered neither happiness nor sadness in me. It only made me more worried, especially when the Sabra and Shatila massacres began a few hours later and it was rumoured that Saad Haddad's soldiers were everywhere in the city looking for revenge. The fear I associated with the massacres was a combination of sadness and jealousy. Sadness for a tragedy that befell innocent civilians, mostly kids and old people un-protected once the Palestinian fighters had been expelled from Lebanon, and jealousy because no one had taken notice of the massacres that preceded Sabra and Shatila. Sabra and Shatila were not presented as the tragic culmination of seven years of indiscriminate killing. On the contrary, they were seen as independent tragedies separate from every-thing that had gone before.

.THREE

But we, like our ideological foes, didn't have much room for conscience. However, while we wanted the war to finish whatever the cost, our foes wanted to keep it going. In pursuing the end of the war, we were ready to freeze our consciences indefinitely. Our foes, pursuing the continuation of the war, put their consciences in yet another separate, refrigerated compartment.

In the meantime I fell in love with the multinationals who had come to Beirut. They became my new political party which would transport me on a magic carpet to a world without wars. The multinationals came from somewhere above and beyond the religious sects. The difference between their multinationalism and our sectarian nationalism was drastic. They – the Americans, the French, the British and the Italians – came from countries that I loved to identify with. Crossing distances was another reason for me to love them. Because those who actually transcend borders are not the only ones to arrive. The people who watch them and derive new ideas from their presence come along as well. They didn't only convince us that the check-points were temporary, they also provided a picture of a world in which there were no checkpoints at all. In our tiny cosmos of Beirut, we were hungry for harmony. The multinationals, with their shaved beards and crisp, ironed clothes, provided it. They came from unimaginable distances, they spoke languages that we had loved to hear in Beirut but which had deserted the city once the war began. Even the civilian non-Lebanese Arabs had left Beirut and we were left alone. But the multinationals quickly discovered that we were warring sects and then they left us as well.

Emigration hit our inner circle. Our few friends began to leave. Joseph started it by going to France, depriving our group of its colour and vitality, giving us the sense of being abandoned in a deserted place. Cruelty was gathering momentum and attacking Beirut once more through 'the war of the mountain', 'the war of the southern suburbs' and 'the war of the camps'. Really, it was tireless barbarity. For two nights my wife Najat and I heard a voice coming from the other side of the wall in the next building where one of the political parties had an office. A man was shouting that he was neither a spy nor a traitor, then he would surrender to cries that made it seem like we were living on the edge of an inferno. It took numerous complaints by people in the building and surrounding neighbourhood to the leader of the party before the office was closed. This was a cruelty that challenged every aspect of our environment.

The problem that my friends and I had with the predominantly Muslim community, which was embroidered with remnants of leftism, was that they wanted to oppose the emergence of a state while we thought it was impossible to oppose something that did not exist. Our problem with the predominantly Christian community was that they were insensitive to what we wanted: a state that represented Muslims fairly and responded to their needs. When it came to the Palestinian factions we wanted arms only in the hands of the legitimate authority. Whereas the problem with the Muslim Shi'ites was that we didn't accept the humiliation of the Palestinians in Lebanon; the problem with the Druze was that we disliked the discrimination against the Christians in the mountains, as much as we hated the Maronite humiliation of the Druze. Those days were the climax of our minority syndrome among a people who were entirely fragmented into microscopic minorities, each one with its own triumphalist majoritarian discourse.

The lira started to lose its value against the dollar, so Joseph offered me a job as a correspondent for a magazine in France. This enabled me to face the hardship of the times, which had been accentuated by my divorce. Love between my wife and me was not enough to overcome the war. So she moved with our daughter Nadoush to her parents' house in East Beirut and I, choosing to return to the dangerous but familiar west, was left alone with darkness.

Beirut then was very dark. Even today, whenever I think of Beirut in the 1980s, I only recall darkness. The city often looked like a huge black block that has been permanently defused. When one walked in its streets one became aware that anything was possible, including a sudden explosion from beneath every stone or behind any silent wall. I used to feel desolation especially when I came home late at night to my huge building and had to ascend five flights of stairs by the light of a single burning match until it scorched my fingers, and another one was struck. When I reached the front door of my flat, I opened it with suspicion as if spirits of some sort were hiding behind it. Night in Beirut became a burden for people who used to love it – yet one can't escape something that returns every twelve hours.

There was also the roar of the electrical generators, and the wires hanging in dangerous and complicated ways between the buildings, the houses and every place else in the street, while the garbage was mounting everywhere, spreading its putrid smell day after day after day. The telephone ceased to function and so did the post office. No one would go to the cinema unless armed or fond of cheap violent films. We almost lost every opportunity to watch a play or go to an exhibition simply because plays and exhibitions were extremely rare. Good songs disappeared and were replaced by kitsch, hastily composed trashy tunes glorifying the 'resistance and steadfastness' in the south. Foreign books became hard currency as did foreign newspapers. So we were all pushed to a primitiveness much like the tune of the constant street clashes. Norms and standards were turned upside down. Contrary to what all schools of architecture say, the best house became the one that was sheltered and least exposed to sun and air because that protected it from shelling. Staying at home became healthier than exercising outside because you might go hoping to improve your body only to come back with a part of it missing. It was also important to keep as far away as possible from cars, whose function had changed. No longer a means of transport, they had become potentially sleeping beasts waiting to explode. And although technology in its long history had created working light switches, which responded the moment they were touched, this stopped as well. You could switch as long as you liked but there was no electricity. You could also turn the tap expecting some hot water, but you'd only get cold. Mind you, most of the time there was no water at all.

We had been pushed downwards to a basic form of survival, familiar to inhabitants of all cities under long sieges. We suddenly became alert when water unexpectedly arrived at four AM, collecting and filling as many empty bottles and containers as possible. Like cavemen, nature governed our lives and times. Myths spread everywhere. One rumour accompanied the drastic decline in the value of the lira. Someone said that anybody who owned certain old coins could exchange them for thousands of dollars. Crowds started gathering in the two Beiruts, each person hoping that he or she would return home a millionaire.

But the real war killed my friend Ali Salamah, a taxi driver who drove south to visit his ageing parents. Ali's face stayed with me for a whole month. He, who hated no one and was never attracted to the business of arms and fighting, always found refuge in the Qur'anic saying: *La haula wala quata ila billah* (No strength, no power but in God).

And when any particular battle dragged on longer than expected we were often hungry. Hasan, Nada and I used to scour forgotten corners of the cupboards in case any tuna, sardines, potatoes or rice had been overlooked. If Zuheir came – Zuheir who knew the militiamen, because he had once been one of them – he was sometimes able to bring us some tinned fish. But even Zuheir couldn't solve all our problems. The steadily declining lira made Hasan consider going to Cyprus to look for work. We were walking at night in the darkened neighbourhood of Verdun, where Abu Samra could count only three lighted houses, when Hasan asked us if we endorsed his plan to emigrate. It was hard for Abu Samra and me to say anything against it. The smell of the burning rubbish made it very difficult to insist that he stay.

Martyrs started to surround us, occupying every available space. They multiplied like mushrooms. Martyr girls, martyr boys, martyr babies, whose fathers took pictures of them and wrote underneath 'the living martyr' in the same way the Iranians did during the war with Iraq. Some said that they raised them specifically to become martyrs. The main headlines on the television news were crowded with living martyrs delivering their messages before launching their operations. They became the most circulated commodity in Beirut. I had not yet learned the beautiful sentence by Cioran: the martyr is a dictator who did not succeed in taking power. If it's so easy for the martyr to kill himself, how easy is it for him to kill me or anyone else? I was overwhelmed by feelings of hate and repugnance for the death that encircled our lives with such frequency. Of course, at the time I didn't have the luxury or the patience to wonder why death had become so popular in Beirut. It was as difficult to ask this question as it was to consider the martyrs simply as dead people who deserved mercy. The necrophiliacs were creeping towards us in a context of unprecedented demographic change. The continuing war in the south and the collapse of its economy and schools changed the whole Beiruti landscape. New symbols replaced old ones. With the rise of Hizbullah, a tent was erected in al-Hamra street, once the most cosmopolitan street in the Middle East, from which martyr hymns and militant statements were broadcast on a daily basis. In an exhibition which Hizbullah presented in the halls of the tourism ministry, there was a fountain of blood. But blood was also spurting in some streets, where butchering sheep on the pavement had suddenly come into vogue.

The city became an extension of the village. Bodies moved in the streets as if in slow motion. People from the countryside who were used to seeing only the cars of their relatives came to Beirut confident that the cars in their rear-view mirrors belonged to their brothers and cousins and would avoid smashing into them. Spatial relationships changed. It became commonplace, for example, to see someone selling cassettes on a make-shift table on wheels, struggling to pass it between two cars with no more than a quarter of a metre between them. People had also lost the ability to exchange social niceties. At the entrances of buildings, it became as difficult to find a man who would ask a woman to enter before him as it was to find a woman who would say 'thank you' if she was encouraged to go first. The façades of buildings constructed in the 1960s in al-Hamra and other streets became an exhibition for clothes that had been washed and hung out to dry. Continuous closures occurred on a daily basis. Today a restaurant is closed, tomorrow a café is going to be closed and the day after a store and so on and so forth. It almost seemed that the main news was about different places closing.

People looked old. Their clothes became tattered and shabby, and even in their imagination, they lost the ability to envision new fashions. Their faces became solid and monolithic, which spoke volumes about a certain constipation of the soul. They began to look so similar, not only in their general demeanours but also in the moustaches and beards which became widespread. All of us lost our ability to be compassionate. Our potential for being kind shrank as our capacity to behave impolitely increased.

Beirut was not the first city to regress to its lumpen suburban roots. Many other places underwent similar relapses. But those who oppressed our city did so in record-breaking time. We were witnesses and victims, and because of this, we became living objects of cruelty; we chose manhood as a feature of Beirut. And indeed it became very manly, like the cities of the hinterlands. The presence of women became less and less evident in the landscape. As the city's essence dried up, its geography was narrowed and trimmed, until a sense of siege enveloped us completely. We used to feel it most acutely when the passages between East and West Beirut were entirely closed. Inside West Beirut, between al-Barbir and al-Raouché, there was a sense that everything was in tatters, which made us think that a divine anger had fallen on us. And yet it was still unacceptable and unfamiliar to be self-critical. We kept refusing to admit that the harm we inflicted on ourselves was equal to the harm inflicted on us by Israel. We learned how violence can function as a beast with two heads, each one nutting the other every now and then, but both of them nutting us on a permanent basis.

Everything was disintegrating – the mental structure, the institutions and civil ethics. A friend of mine who taught at the Lebanese University showed me some papers written by his students. One of them called Freud 'a filthy degenerate'. Another saw Max Weber as an agent of imperialism conspiring against Muslims. This was not so strange when we remember that some militant professors cancelled the regular courses and started teaching Islamic heritage instead of anthropology, Arab discourse instead of psychology and *hakawati* (local popular theatre) instead of Shakespeare.

The militiamen overstretched their hospitality to foreigners by kidnapping them. This was another blow to 'our' reputation. But it was not only a question of image, it was a matter of reality. If the foreigners were the first victims, we were second in a long queue. At the end of every week, I had to go to the crossing between the two Beiruts in order to pick up my daughter so she could spend her weekends in the west of the city. Or I would go to be with her in the east. But it was becoming more and more difficult. Sniping often made it necessary for the crossings to change location, and we were constantly discovering new ones by following the footprints through the muddied alleyways. My comings and goings between the two sectors of Beirut were more than just a personal challenge. During my journeys, some of the pale, bearded faces I used to see looked as if they hadn't been exposed to the sun for ages. They resembled the way I imagined the kidnappers: standing in small groups of four or five each; their eyes piercing; their hair unkempt; their beards left as nature intended. But those who call themselves 'resisters to Israel' were also responsible for many mini-wars among themselves.

And after each of their battles I used to check the city streets accompanied by Waddah. We used to examine the areas that had been hit by the shelling, observing the changes and the damage. We behaved like someone counting his personal losses as if the city was our property. Many times we exhausted our memories in order to establish what had disappeared. But checking the streets with Waddah was also fun and sometimes consoling. Because concentrating on the devastation took us beyond both the conflict and the immediate location. Free-association transported us to places, writings and films from which we could view our destruction as a mere moment in wider context. During these times, we used to celebrate the publishing of a book by one of our few friends and this compensated a tiny bit for our misery.

Some of us had lost all connections with our relatives in the countryside because the roads had been cut between Beirut and the rest of Lebanon. Thus the links of friendship became a substitute for family relations. It was as if we were almost living together in a commune. Sometimes when a militia clash erupted, we ended up sleeping in the house in which we were spending the evening. If the electricity was cut in a certain neighbourhood, we would simply stay where there was light. Gradually friendships ceased to be a free choice, they evolved into rituals. We became like a party cell which couldn't co-exist with anyone outside it and couldn't listen to any talk that was not its own.

I don't know if we knew happiness in those years. But I'm sure we knew fun. We laughed every now and then, and amused ourselves. I remembered this recently when I read Milan Kundera's criticism of ex-dissidents in Czechoslovakia, those who recall only the misery of politics and forget the moments of celebration. We were pushed to adventure without searching for it. We had already passed through our youth and had finished experimenting when war came to us. We didn't need, or expect, a test for our bodies and souls, but it came anyway. Shelling ceased to move our desires but between one terrible Israeli bombing wave and the next we enjoyed some of the most delicious drinks we ever drank. We drank like people who had just returned from the gates of death.

We waited a long time for the end of the war and we counted the days like people sitting on chairs without changing their shirts or washing their faces. Old age started to attack us while stupidity, which consumed the city, provoked us to the point that we lost the distinction between the provoked and the provoker. They merged to a point after which I could only see things from a specific angle and in a particular position. Instead of considering stupidity as a reason for empathy I went too far in political dogma and judgmentalism.

Of course I was wrong, but everything was obscured by the overwhelming darkness which overshadowed personal events, intermingling and confusing them to the point at which they became irredeemably entangled. It was impossible to emerge with a strong memory and it continued to be so as the parallel guilty feelings kept growing. Then someone phoned me, telling me to come to London where there was work waiting for me. So, to London then.

CONFESSIONS OF
A TARAB ADDICT

Kamal Kassar

Layla Murad

A couple of years after graduating from law school I fell in love with a voice that belonged to the singer Marie Jubran. I bought all of her recordings, and listened to them night and day. She was a mezzo-soprano who sang *tarab*. Her renditions of the old songs were wonderful. During the first year of my marriage, I remember sleeping with the cassette between my head and my wife's, listening to Jubran and wondering, 'What was she like?' Then one day a man who was a radio director came to me with his legal problems. We also talked about the old actors we knew from cinema because he had known them as young actors in radio. When I found out that he knew Jubran, I insisted he describe her eyes, her nose, her hair, her body, how she used to sing. He told me many stories. In Damascus where she was living, the churches, to celebrate the Easter feast, used to invite a big orchestra from abroad, and she would sing. I was proud that this very important *tarab* singer was also a soloist. The radio director said she was beautiful, and that an Italian pianist from one of the orchestras fell in love with her and tried to commit suicide, after she turned him down. I was intrigued. Nobody knew about Jubran; she just disappeared. Despite this huge legacy of *tarab*, singers fade away; they're forgotten. Since then, I've felt it was my duty to contribute to spreading their influence through time, and across borders.

.THE ENCHANTMENT OF THE DEVIL

One of my early memories of music was an Egyptian song that captivated me when I was around eight years old. I must have heard it on the radio. Because of this song, I was in a state of desperate love. It was always in my head, and I never knew why. Many years later when I finally returned to Beirut after the civil war, this same song –'*Sanateen Wana Hayel Feek*' (For Two Years Now, You've Driven Me Mad) by Layla Murad, a renown *tarab* singer and actress who was the daughter of the Egyptian composer Zaki Murad – popped into my head again. I immediately ran into a cassette shop, sang the song to the guy behind the counter, and he gave it to me. It was my first encounter with Beirut after spending eight years living in Paris.

I had returned to Beirut in 1999 with a big appetite for this music. Once the singer Abdel-Karim Al-Chaar brought me some rare *tarab* recordings he made in Syria and Egypt, we started collecting together. Historically the main capitals for *tarab* were Aleppo (and Damascus) and Cairo, where we found archive radio broadcasts, old films – an important source for the music since songs were per-formed live in the movies but weren't recorded elsewhere – and amateur recordings. In our travels, we discovered a network of *tarab* lovers who were also *tarab* dealers. But the network has its drawbacks. There is no real method of working, and many of the dealers have more or less the same material. Usually it is of a poor quality, since many of the performances were recorded in bad conditions. There are technical reasons for this, but there was also something else: nobody knows when an artist will sing wonderfully because *tarab* is something formed in an instance of 'giftness'.

Outstanding *tarab* performances usually take place in cafés, houses or weddings — rarely in recording studios. Not even the tracks on the CDs and LPs of Umm Kulthum are her best ones. Those songs were chosen because they were short and technically good. The *tarab* network trades in rare recordings of Umm Kulthum, and these are different from what's normally available. So *tarab* dealers can, in effect, make you more addicted to *tarab*! Abu Ayman, an old man living in Damascus, opened an old, thick notebook when we visited him. The entries described every Umm Kulthum concert. There were columns for the date of the concert, where it took place, the names of the songs, and an additional column for 'Remarks'. This column was mainly blank except that the word 'devil' had been periodically written in pencil.

When I asked about that, Abu Ayman explained that those were the times that Umm Kulthum was inhabited by the 'devil' — meaning she was not normal. I was amazed and bought every 'devil-inhabited' recording of hers that he had. His use of the word 'devil' made me think of *duende* from Spain, when a performer, whether singing, dancing or bullfighting, is inhabited by a *jinn*. In *tarab*, a singer can be transformed. In the music, someone like Umm Kulthum is caught between two states of consciousness.

It could be said that Umm Kulthum took us by the hand to *tarab*. She was a phenomenon beyond music. Besides the power of her voice, she represented the pinnacle of the conjunction between politics and culture. In the 1960s, Gamal Abdul Nasser was the charismatic, living embodiment of Arab nationalism.

He loved Umm Kulthum, and Umm Kulthum loved him. Together they were cataclysmic when it came to Arab self-identity. So when I was growing up in Beirut, I experienced something that's only written about in books today. On every first Thursday of the month, you wouldn't find a cat on the street: everybody was mesmerized, listening to her new concert on Radio Cairo. If, however, you were running late and happened to be caught outside, you still heard the concert since all the windows were wide open and the volume loud.

Of course, she had the best composers/singers – the kings of tarab from the 1940s, 1950s and 1960s, people like Zakariyya Ahmad, Dawud Husni, Muhammad Al-Qasabji, Riyad Al-Sumbati and not least Muhammad 'Abdel-Wahab. Tarab existed before Umm Kulthum, but the singers were repetitive. They would follow a melodic mode and sing for hours. Umm Kulthum, her composers and her poets, introduced tarab to new generations, and it is this popularity that remains with us today. She is still our 'Empress'.

Why don't you see the stars in daylight? It is because the sun is so bright. The Kawkab Ash-sharq (Star of the East) was so powerfully bright that all the other stars living at the same time were hardly visible. The more I search now, the more I find that there were many good tarab singers and songs during Umm Kulthum's career, but her tarab blotted them out. I feel that it is essential to bring them to light.

.SCREENING THE PAST
One of the aims of a developed society is to screen the past and take possession of its history, so its culture and people are well-known. In underdeveloped countries, the opposite occurs. I remember asking my sister-in-law every time she went to Egypt to look for the recordings by the singer Fathiya Ahmad from the 1950s and early 1960s. She was Egyptian, living in Egypt and was so famous that she was known as Mutribat al-Qutrain (Singer of Two Lands), yet nobody remembers anything about her. 'Is she Moroccan or Lebanese? Is she a dancer?' inquired the vendors.

While I was training to be a lawyer in 1972, I was sent to get a man out of jail, there I contracted viral hepatitis B. I was in hospital for two or three weeks, followed by five months in bed. It was tough, but I read a book a day and had a small radio recorder to keep me occupied. Every evening at five or six o'clock, I tuned to this wonderful Arabic singing on Israel radio. It seems that the majority of musicians in Iraq were Jews, who left for Israel in the 1960s. I recorded them from my sick bed, along with lots of other local music from Kuwait and Bahrain. I made copies, and sent them to friends. Then when I was living in Paris, I found virtually every Arabic record released (because everything goes to Paris), but I became aware of the lack of information about the singers and the musicians. Had they been playing western classical music, there would have been ample literature and critical reviews, but local popular musical cultures like tarab are not well documented. Whenever I find a new singer or a recording, it reminds me of the mammoth job that still lies ahead.

In 1973, Umm Kulthum gave a concert in Baalbek, which may have been her last public performance. The sound engineer had placed microphones all around the orchestra. My friend and singer Abdel-Karim Al-Chaar unofficially plugged in his tape recorder and captured what later appeared to be something amazing. The raw, unedited recording reveals Umm Kulthum as an old woman who was starting to forget her lines. But her faithful musicians were there to back her, singing along when necessary or extending their musical space, giving her time to remember. What this recording shows is how much Umm Kulthum and her orchestra had become a single entity. It is not astonishing to see them dying, one after the other, very soon after she passed away. When her composer and *oud* player Al-Qasabji died, she refused to replace him, leaving his seat on stage unoccupied. And when Muhammad Abdo Saleh died, she installed his *qanun* (Arabic zither) on his seat in front of the audience. This recording is indeed one of these rare treasures that archivists would kill for.

.ROOTS AND ROUTES

The origins of *tarab* date back to the beginning of the Islamic conquest when the troops went north towards Syria. During this period Mecca, one of the stops on the caravan trail, was witnessing a peaceful and prosperous life, and the wealthy people there were entertained by singing slave girls, most of them Persians. Two in particular, 'Azzat al-Mayla and Jamíla are remembered in historical accounts for their concerts in Meccan homes, where they sang Persian songs. Both music from Persia and Byzantium were the early, big influences on Arabic music, as was a local, pre-Islamic musical tradition from northern Syria, northern-western Iran and Iraq and southern Turkey, a region inhabited by the oldest Christian tribes on earth. The Islamization of these remote areas brought

many local musical traditions to the very heart of the religion, the evidence of which can be found in the variations in the singing of the Qur'an throughout the Middle East and North Africa. In the Levant, Islam was formed by Persian, Byzantine and local Christian musical influences. In Morocco it was influenced by Berber traditions.

Recently, I showed a video I made of the Zurkhani in Isfahan, Iran, to a young Beiruti filmmaker. The Zurkhani is a rhythmical gymnastic, performed to the rhythms and songs of a ritualistic music with drums and bells, to accompany a group of men exercising in a traditional gymnasium. The young filmmaker, who was watching the video with me, suddenly shouted out, 'That is Assyriac!' The melodies of the Iranian Zurkhani singer were the same melodies sung in Assyrian churches. *Tarab* lives in a place where a major encounter of civilizations is still taking place, and that's what gives the music its special richness and enlightenment.

What Islam did was to codify the transmission of the singing and recitation of the Qur'an, in effect freezing the language. Today, youngsters studying to become religious sheikhs are still taught the same way they were hundreds of years ago. Because of this, local musics remain ingrained in Islamic liturgy. Both Aleppo and Cairo have the best Qur'anic singing due to the influence of Byzantine Greek music.

Up until the 1960s, the sheikhs with the greatest voices, who recited the Qur'an in the al-Hussein Mosque in Cairo, used to meet, along with a few *tarab* addicts, in one of the rooms of the great edifice. There they would sing love and longing songs for the benefit of those who would experience the most exquisite enjoyment from this art form. I am thrilled to have some of the rare recordings from these sessions.

When someone sings *tarab,* he has a motif. It could be a couple of verses of a traditional poem or a few words by an unknown author. This singer takes this motif, and god only knows where it will lead. It could lead him to nothing, to a loop, but then again, it could lead the singer and everyone listening to felicity or enchantment. This is called *samad,* a Sufi word which I suspect has some connection to the Hindu *samadi. Samadi* is a high degree of experience. The Sufi experienced *samad,* and the performer – when he is in the throes of the 'devil' or *duende* – is *sultanising* – raising himself and everyone else to a high level! The audience experiences *samad,* an intensity of spiritual pleasure – something that can't be duplicated because it occurs completely unexpectedly in the music.

Nour El Huda

.TARAB IS FEELING

This emotional elevation takes place despite the rigid system of *maqamat* or melodic modes in Arabic music. In the west, there is one major mode and one minor mode. In Arabic music, there are sixty to ninety modes that are most commonly used, although hundreds of thousands are said to exist. Singers usually stick closely to one mode because any deviation is often construed as singing out of key, but how boring to stay in one mode and go up or down like Persian classical music, where some instruments are tuned to one mode only.

Sheikh Ahmad Habboush

Brightness comes when modes are associated and a bridge leads from one mode to another. Then in that melody, at a certain degree, a note can cross into yet another melody. The virtuoso singer or instrumentalist knows these secrets, which aren't taught in the conservatory, although they can be learned from a generous teacher. Probably Umm Kulthum's father gave her certain musical recipes, in the same way Samir Sibliui, the professor from the Lebanese National Music Conservatory, in Beïrut, who is teaching me the *nay* (reed flute), tells me some of the secrets of playing Arabic music. He would say, if you're playing the E quarter-tone, quarter-flat – for the Turkish effect, you have to push it a little more. For the Egyptian effect, push it another way, but it's not a sharp. This is not the wherefore and the science of music, it has to do with feeling; and when you are playing, it's too late to perform what you're thinking about.

Have you ever had the chance to listen to that unique recording of Nour El Huda singing a cappella *'Ya Garatal Wadi'* (O Neighbour of the Valley). The lyrics of this famous song were composed by 'Abdel-Wahab after a poem written by the Egyptian poet Ahmad Shawki, known as 'the Prince of Poets'. *'Ya Garatal Wadi'* has been interpreted by 'Abdel-Wahab himself as well as by the Lebanese singer Fayruz, and soon it became very popular throughout the Arab World. Yet only a few *tarab* seekers listened to the outstanding, full of emotion and *duende* version of El Huda. One of the best voices in my opinion, El Huda was sadly forsaken and she passed away, cruelly ignored, lonely and penniless.

Tarab is feeling, and *tarab* singers and players know the path towards enchantment. They are magicians, but they are not geishas. They are real lovers; they have their own personal involvement with the music. Some have enough science to pretend to feel the emotions, but the singers who are truly involved have an aura, and the audience can feel it in the music. I've experienced the '*tarab* moment' when I went to a house in Aleppo and heard a concert by the impressive, young Sheikh Ahmad Habboush. I've also experienced it during concerts given by Abdel-Karim Al-Chaar.

.ABDEL-KARIM AL-CHAAR AND HIS TWO DAUGHTERS
Abdel-Karim grew up in a Muslim-Christian family in Tripoli. When he was young, his father was assassinated because he was a Communist, and according to his son, because he had married a Christian. So the father's family took the small boy away from his mother, and placed him with his older brothers who were studying to become religious sheikhs. Early on, his fine singing voice made him popular in the mosques, where he didn't study as much as sing and recite the Qur'an. Periodically though, he escaped to his mother's village of Batrumeen, where he attended long, orthodox Christian masses in the local cathedral and learned to sing canticles, or non-metrical hymns, and Christian liturgy. But he was always forced back home to Tripoli by his older, stricter brothers. Abdel-Karim says he had a sad childhood because he knew that the animosity his father's family felt towards his mother was the cause of his father's death.

As a singer, Abdel-Karim has had a uniquely personal experience with music. He has the bigness of Oriental

Muhammad Khayri

culture inside him, and this is the inheritance he received from his sad childhood and the special combination of the musical influences to which he was exposed. As a performer, Abdel-Karim is always involved. He's an adventurer, and people criticise him for taking risks. I remember one of the largest concerts held in the UNESCO concert hall when he was singing. Suddenly he stopped and told the band to start again. He was on a musical path and could go no further. But then there have been other performances where his singing flows majestically.

Abdel-Karim has two daughters, Raneen and Reem, and both have wonderful voices with different qualities and personalities. He wanted to teach them how to sing, but I argued against that. Abdel-Karim was born in a special environment where he was breathing music without realising it was already living and growing inside him. His daughters are not in the same situation and they cannot reach his heights simply through his instruction. I suggested that they go to the music conservatory in Tripoli to learn the 'how' of music – another way of gaining the father's knowledge. Both of them are doing that now. Reem, the younger sister, is also learning the qanun, another route to greater musical understanding.

Today, many young tarab singers find it difficult to make a living. There is an enormous pressure on them to sing commercially because the new sound is digitised Arabic pop, and producers overlook singers who have been trained in a more traditional manner. However, tarab remains a living, popular musical tradition, meaning that the music is still sung and sought after by a hungry audience. What's needed is the means to bring the two – the young singers and the devoted audience – together, perhaps through a new compilation release of contemporary tarab. To use a musical allegory, tarab is Arabic blues; it is the emotional wail and the instinctual, heartfelt response that still underpins much of the musical culture in the modern Middle East.

.FORGOTTEN VOICES
One day I phoned Abdel-Karim after hearing a very, very bad recording of songs by a singer I didn't recognise. I had become interested in a set of old songs that are rhythmically alert and joyful, performed by Syrian artists. In these bad recordings, there was one real tarab singer. His grainy voice had texture and nuance. He was singing the same songs as Sabah Fakhri – people know Fakhri, a popular singer of qudud halabiah, a mixture of local Aleppan old songs, chansonette and mowashah, a style of singing from eleventh or twelfth century Andalucía – but Fakhri seemed aerobic in comparison. Later I learned that the singer was Muhammad Khayri, allegedly one of Fakhri's teachers, who never recorded CDs or LPs, but had a plethora of cassettes. Eventually I met musicians who played with him, and they told me he was totally unpredictable, an alcoholic who sang with his back towards the audience. Despite everything, he always gave very good performances.

Abdel-Karim and I started trying to improve the sound quality of all the recordings of Khayri's concerts we managed to get hold of. We were particularly keen on a concert that took place in the Assabeel Garden, in

Aleppo, from the 1970s. It was a terrible recording of a bad loudspeaker in the garden. At that time they used to put a lot of echo on recordings and the percussion was too close to the microphone. It was a nightmare but Abdel-Karim and I spent weeks cleaning it up on the computer.

.THE DILEMMAS OF AN ARCHIVIST

Initially, I was disappointed by the sound quality of original *tarab* recordings; one has to imagine 60 per cent of the song to understand what it was like. Moreover, the software for cleaning up tracks was not effective, with at best only 10 or 20 per cent improvement in sound quality. It's been an upward learning curve, but computer programmes like ProTools, popular among western pop or rock musicians recording in their garages or bedrooms, have given me more hope of recapturing *tarab*'s original sound and excitement.

In the meantime, I've been asking myself, if I improve these songs and put them on a CD, what's next? Should I be proud when people come to my house and I play it for them? That's too much like the dealers I've met in the *tarab* network. Some people have a small collection of a particular singer, or their parents were fond of somebody, and they keep their recordings, but they don't make copies for other people. It's as if they're saying, 'You don't have what I have, but you can come and listen to it – only with me.'

This reminds me of the mentality of mathematicians in the seventeenth century. They made discoveries, but they wouldn't say what they were. I feel that we need to have access to those collections, in the same way, people with a real interest in the music should have access to my collection. One of the recordings that I cherish in particular is a concert given by Sheikh Al-Fishni in the al-Hussein mosque in Cairo, in 1973. He sang for the troops the night before they left to fight Israel. It is a breathtaking concert but such incredible music shouldn't be for myself alone. Ideally, there should be an association that will give *tarab* back to the Arab world either through a series of new CDs or at least a collection or an archive, which is open to the public.

In my life, I have experienced some real moments of discovery while listening to music. When I first heard the Japanese flute, I said to myself, 'I knew this existed; I knew it would be like this.' I had the same epiphany when I heard gamelan for the first time in Jakarta. It's as if there are these compartments in your brain ready to receive music. Music gives a huge amount of pleasure, because the best kind of pleasure is the pleasure of the mind.

Kamal Kassar was interviewed by Malu Halasa.

WARMILK

Zeina B. Ghandour

.WAR

Early in the days of the last century, there passed through Beirut one of those English travellers who felt better in the east. Clear misfits at home, these well-born ladies and gentleman were beguiled by the Orient. And these amateurs, both men and women, give a lot of us the creeps. Particularly liberals in the west, and Patriots, Fundamentalists and Pan-Arabists in the east, are united in feeling their skin crawl at the mention of their names. Because a lot of them did not stop at sketching desert oases by day and listening to live, improvised poetry by moonlight. Some took to politics, and sought to influence the course of history. To that end they spoke with two tongues, and bewitched us with proclamations of Arab unity, just as they betrayed us with their treaties.

Even though undeniably romantic, they were business people at heart and we were, to them, the colourful spoils of war.

But this one English traveller had a particular presence of mind, and his inexhaustible reserves of charm turned the tides of the desert across the Jordan in his favour. His flair for a good raid wrecked the day for many a Turk, and his self-effacing masochism belied his actual sphere of influence. Rabble-rousing consort to resplendent Hejazi emirs, map-maker, matinee idol, guerrilla commander of the unruly tribes of the interior, there was only ever one, ruling, inimitable Orientalist. And this is what he said:

> Beyrout is the door of Syria, with a Levantine screen through which shop-soiled foreign influences flow into Syria. It is as representative of Syria as Soho of the Home Counties, and yet in Beyrout, from its geographical position, from its schools, from the freedom engendered by intercourse with many foreigners, there was a nucleus of people, Mohammedans, talking and writing and thinking like the doctrinaire cyclopaedists who paved the way for revolution in France, and whose words permeated to parts of the interior where action is in favour. For their sake … and for the power of its wealth, and for its exceeding loud and ready voice, Beyrout is to be reckoned with.
> T.E. Lawrence, afterwards Shaw, Arab Bulletin 12 March 1917,
> Secret Despatches from Arabia

Not much has changed. T.E. was onto something. But just in case that wasn't enough, then keep it locked, there's more.

.MILK

Grandma's apartment is full of treasures. Let me list the kitchen booty. First, the classic pickles: baby aubergines stuffed with walnuts and chillies, drenched in oil. Then, the acquired taste: molasses that she will mix later with tahini for me, to be scooped up with bread and line my anglicized stomach with cement. This year's olive harvest maturing in tall jars with pieces of lemon. Lined up in the pantry, for an utterly fragrant thirst-quencher, the oily bottles of rose water. Orange water for our rice pudding. Dates from Arabia, rolled in cumin seeds. Thyme tea from Egypt. Truffles from Syria the size of grapefruits, only recently unearthed. Jordanian *zaatar* for breakfast with tomatoes and warmed bread. Spicy, paper-thin, bite-size pizza for us to reheat from the freezer when she doesn't feel like cooking for me, to nibble on whilst watching *Lawrence of Arabia* on DVD (again). Pistachio-laden *halawa* that melts on first contact with tongue. And chocolate everywhere, Cadbury's and Leonida and Reese's, in the cupboards, in the fridge, in the dining room and in the bedroom.

Food for the firm-hearted. When it comes to food, we don't flounder or flinch. This is how we are folkloric, steadfast. Before I could visit Beirut again, and renew acquaintance with this regal old lady who is my grandmother, all these delicacies and more regularly travelled to my adoptive London, in suitcases dragged by my mother. Every time we, her children, laughed at the content, ridiculed the stock whilst marvelling at how nothing ever spilled or leaked. We laughed so as not to appear nostalgic, even as we brimmed over with nostalgia.

Grandma wears her amber-tinted outsize sunnies indoors in the afternoon, when the rays are long. 'Your mother was always so delicate,' she says. 'The first time she moved inside me, she fluttered, like a butterfly.' *Zay el farashe.* Her blue threaded hands rest on her abdomen. I can't see her eyes, but the atmosphere is light, the sadness latent.

Their migration from Africa has brought a flock of pink birds to the Corniche. It's April in Beirut and I stroll, luxuriating in a rain-soaked breeze. As the sun dips into the horizon, I wonder what it would have been like, does anyone remember, to have hopped on to the train to Haifa from here?

.WAR

The desert adventurers then, of whom T.E. was the most flamboyant and most literary representative, were a hardy breed, one that had been starved of spirituality and tenderness. They were children weaned by strangers, and they formed the Empire's backbone.

What they loved most was authenticity in an Arab, and held in some contempt the tinctured townsfolk of Beirut, Damascus and Cairo, with their half-baked western ideas. They looked down on most aspects of Levantinism, and loved the Bedouin better, for their freedom from choice and civilization.

> *The Moslems were divided rather sharply into the intelligentsia and the Arabs. The first were those who had thrown off Arab things, and bared themselves to the semi-Levantine, semi-European fashions of the renegade Moslem – the Moslem who had lost his traditional faith – and with it all belief in all faiths.*
> *T.E., War Diaries*

And that's just the Moslems.

True to fashion, T.E. championed the dashing camel riders of western Arabia and in so doing, made an example of himself to the Bedou. He led by example, sought to inspire with self-inflicted pain and deprivation, and sublimated his physical needs to the redeeming transcendence of political engagement. At the same time he had an erotic appeal to be reckoned with. He wore the most dazzling white robes, and he had blue eyes for days …

Of all this, it's fair to say, the savvy Bedou took heed. T.E. made their acquaintance as no one else, and went so deep under cover in Arabia, that his wayward behaviour started to cause disquiet among the ranks. Was he an Englishman playing with the Nomad, or a Nomad playing with the English? The head of the French Military Mission who was sent down to liaise with him, immediately assessed him as off the rails or in his own words, a 'case for a psychiatrist'.

By all accounts, and especially by his own writings, it appears that T.E. was indeed a bit soppy. But this is to underestimate him, for he never lost sight of his mission, never wavered in his watchful objectivity, and his observations will regale the most assiduous student of anthropology:

To choke at a meal, through taking too large a handful, is the most serious breach of manners possible, and stops the feast. A Shammar chief who choked, slit his cheek with a dagger from his mouth, and showed the people that the meat was caught on his tooth, not too large to swallow. In the Hejaz, the diners break up together from the food. In the Northern Arabs each man rises as he is filled. The Fedaan like the guest to eat in the dark, and by himself, that he may not be ashamed of his appetite.
War Diaries, January 1917

He was himself ashamed of his own appetite, and saw a healthy one in others as a sign of moral feebleness. He had deemed the young Emir Abdullah too much of a *bon viveur* to be of any use as a leader to the Arabs, finding his tent too luxuriously carpeted, his table too well supplied. *Abdullah would ride a little, shoot a little, then return to his tent for massage,* he wrote. The twinkle in his eye and his endless pranks made him look like a bit of a playboy. Feisal, on the other hand, unlike his lazy no-good brother, was sufficiently austere, and his mere demeanour drove T.E. to declare that he was made of the mettle of prophets. A committed chain-smoker, Feisal was duly noted to play with his food absent-mindedly until he could wave it away once his guests had had their fill.

If there is a link between renunciation and greed, it can be regularly found in the prototype of a British colonial personality. And this is how it came that T.E. glimpsed in the refutation of food and all bodily comforts, the potential for achieving integrated spiritual leadership.

But meanwhile he was so hungry, he was growing fangs.

.MILK

Sometimes Grandma refuses to eat, or at least pretends to have lost her appetite. Obstinate and resolute, these stretches of non-compliance can be a bit of a haul for those around her. At times like these she and I organize the silence. Our communication acquires a cinematic quality, as we shuffle from room to room, tinker with the heating and the blinds, boil water for tea that we don't drink, connect and disconnect the radio, drag pillows around, sit around a lot and say very little. I know Grandma is suffering, that her suffering is metaphysical, and that I must suffer with her in solidarity. I'm reminded how alike we are and take it for a blessing. *Baraka*.

'Teta,' she tells me as we stand brushing our teeth in her bathroom, 'Do you know how many years it's been since I've looked at myself in the mirror? Five, maybe six.' She wipes her mouth with a towel, while holding on to the door. 'Sometimes I can't believe this decaying lump of flesh is really me.' Grandma's English is impeccable, the World Service her constant companion.

I come to recuperate the knowledge that migrates across generations, and to be uplifted. I come to turn the table on the male artists in this world, and to champion my own muse. I come to drink from her well, and to reveal my source. All the culture I need is within these four walls. I come to harness her goodness and to lap it up. With her, it's down and rootsy, in a visceral, intractable way.

When she's officially off food, Grandma is indomitable. She will not be told and she will not be humoured. Anything that comes her way must be spurned. She becomes antisocial, antiseptic, antibiotic. If you're in the mood for a crushing tongue-lashing, then it's worth gently prodding her. She will invoke on demand the catalogue of ills which conspire to defeat her appetite. She has a lump in her throat, her mouth is dry. She can't chew the meat, it's too tough. The state of the market vegetables is pitiful, the onions are mouldy, the lemons dry. The bread breaks off and crumbles because of the way it's packaged. The grapes taste of pesticide. She can't sit down long enough for a meal, because her ankles are swollen and she must keep her legs raised. Her beloved cook, Umm Khodor, can't cook and never could. Her rice is too starchy and her stews over-stewed. But she doesn't begrudge her for it: even at her harshest, Grandma's stellar kindness glows on and on.

Still, in the interest of peace and harmony, the subject is best changed. The truth is, she will, in the end, eat. In the meantime she must be allowed to subvert the system in her own way, to demolish the convenient cuddly grandma myth. And for the rebellious streak of this unladylike conceit, I love her all the more.

Suffice it to say that these episodes can stretch out indefinitely and apply even to chocolate which, between one visit and the next, acquires the dusty glaze of third-world imports.

.WAR

The dark creature had made a dark journey into the heart of self-denial, and rediscovered pleasure. He grew attached to sensations unmediated by man, began to appreciate water over wine and to reject the outer emblems of power. T.E. had always been into 'street Arabs', and here he was again, keeping it Real.

War became prayer. Pain a source of inspiration and thanksgiving. A complex relationship between the poet and nature developed, endurance led to a communion with the spirits. He took on the qualities of the desert wind, its power and invisibility.

El hawa sultan. Normally unflappable, the shamanic Bedou fell under the spell of the martyr.

But T.E.'s *materia pura* were not only killer Bedouins, they were also Bedouin killers, whose blood feuds and family grudges threatened to undermine the design of war. As a strategist he took heed of two factors: that the Bedou loved nothing more than loot and plunder, and that his rag-tag assembly of hot-heads would not hesitate to regulate a long-standing enmity in a bit of 'blue on blue', or friendly fire. Forget your enemies, a forlorn T.E. had once declared, it's your friends who can really damage you.

The reconciliation of the tribes to each other for the sake of the Arab Movement then, was turned into a feature of the Arab Revolt. It became known as Feisal's Peace, but really it was none other than *pax Britannica*, and it was implemented with the inventive use of local customary law. With T.E. sitting on their councils, the tribes fell in line with each other. T.E. was then able to fully exploit their genius for guerrilla warfare, and in this way Wejh was taken, Medina put under siege, Akaba gloriously claimed, and the road to Damascus cleared.

Feisal, for the time being at least, had gone clear. But when they pulled up together and triumphant at the Jordan as the right flank of Allenby's army, it was T.E.'s messianic optimism which was the greater. Like the three thousand prophets who had gone before him, he emerged from the desert ready to preach salvation.

When Lawrence returned to England after the war, changed his name to Shaw and joined the Royal Air Force, he was asked by a superior why he had enlisted. He replied, '*I think I must have had a mental breakdown, Sir.*' It's not really surprising, for he had made some fundamental mistakes. He had taken war for an amorous adventure, and himself for an avatar.

.MILK

When I went away to university, and it was before email, my mother used to sign her handwritten letters to me, Your Mother. At the time it felt glacial. It was only years later that I regained my mother tongue, and the tenderness which frosted over in translation.

Ummuki.

I want to live somewhere where people cry upon arrival and departure.

The reruns of my first return keep gaining in pathos. All the while the arrivals terminal at Beirut International gets shinier, the nightlife flashier, the pavements busier, the buildings newer. I look at Beirut with extra-terrestrial vision, and see it sparkle from space.

Thai, Japanese, Vietnamese restaurants. Jazz bars, blues bars, Irish pubs, pseudo-Ottoman evening entertainment. Flourishing gay scene. Decadent beach life, avant-garde architecture, political satire on television. Feminist discussion on the Hizbullah channel. Sexually permissive atmosphere. My driver on this occasion has a guru in India. International conferences on peace-building, foreign investment. Non-governmental initiatives on reconciliation, institutionalized healing. Some remaining clues after all, of our collective depravity. Forget your enemies, T.E. had said, it's your friends who hurt you.

How can we heal, whilst refusing to assess the damage?

Outside I tread on eggshells. The surface of lies is so heavy, it threatens to crush my heart. It takes sustained frantic activity to silence the stones, and stifle the scenes they've registered. I fear the first energetic lull, when they might transmit the memory, the guilt.

Amongst the rubble and the concrete blocks, my nomad's mind won't settle. I wonder if the imaginary tattoo I've given myself is visible, a circle of blue dots, right on my chin. In Beirut I feel conspicuous, provincial. Knowing urbanite yearns for the unknowing of the desert. I transmute into an English traveller, shunning the atheism and materialism of the oriental city. Have I become another European doctrinaire, was Arabic ever my mother tongue?

At Grandma's, we pore over old photographs, newspaper cuttings, frayed prints. She spreads them out across the coffee table and I inch towards her slightly on the sofa, to better catch her vibe. Shabby road map for an excursion into the past. It's an annual ritual that refuses to tire. A young woman with long black tresses smiles wryly for the photographer. It's my aunt, relaxing in the outdoors with her anti-establishment friends. Even by the standards of today, her demeanour is defiant. The men around her sport sideburns and flares, their guns are casually strewn amongst the picnicware. They're from the local Fateh crew, representing the PLO Massive. They're here on sufferance, and here on business. Confident and cool, their timeless appeal is ammunition for the struggle.

Grandma especially likes this photograph.

© Zeina B. Ghandour 2003

AT HOME

Reine Mahfouz

Reine Mahfouz's photographs of kitchens and backyards could be from Tuscany or Pennsylvania. Rustic chic, they recall bygone days when people lived simply, close to the land. Interestingly these pictures are from Palestinian refugee camps in Lebanon. Mahfouz started going to the refugee camps in 1998 when she was still a university student. The first time she went with her friends, and a camera, she was thrown out. The second time she was told she needed a permit to take pictures. Eventually she ended up in Burj el-Barajneh near Beirut's airport, where she photographed people and children in the streets. 'My first project was a process of discovery, but that was only the first layer,' she explains.

Mahfouz was born in East Beirut, the Christian side of the city, where the Palestinians are routinely blamed for the country's civil war. Curiosity and determination kept her going back to the camps, where she noticed the appalling conditions Palestinians live in. 'They are not allowed to work in Lebanon. The Lebanese government also prevents them from restoring homes or building new ones, allegedly "supporting the Palestinian fight to return to the motherland". The situation on the ground is different: there are relatively few young men in the camps because most of them have gone to Europe, looking for work. As a result, the women end up doing men's jobs, some of which is hard labour, like fixing or constructing houses.'

As a photographer, Mahfouz was acutely aware of the stereotypic way in which the Palestinians are re-presented in photojournalism. Then one day she saw sunlight on the pots and pans while looking in on a kitchen, and thought, 'This really has nothing to do with the way we normally visualize the camps. I wanted to capture something different in the details of the plants on the stairs or a curtain hanging from a window, but even then I couldn't get away from the reality of the camps. The swings in the park, where the children play, are riddled with bullet holes.'

Palestinian refugee home-owners were a little surprised at what Mahfouz wanted to photograph, but over the years they have gotten used to her, and regard her as a friend. Her unusual photographs capture the quiet power of self-reliance.

Malu Halasa

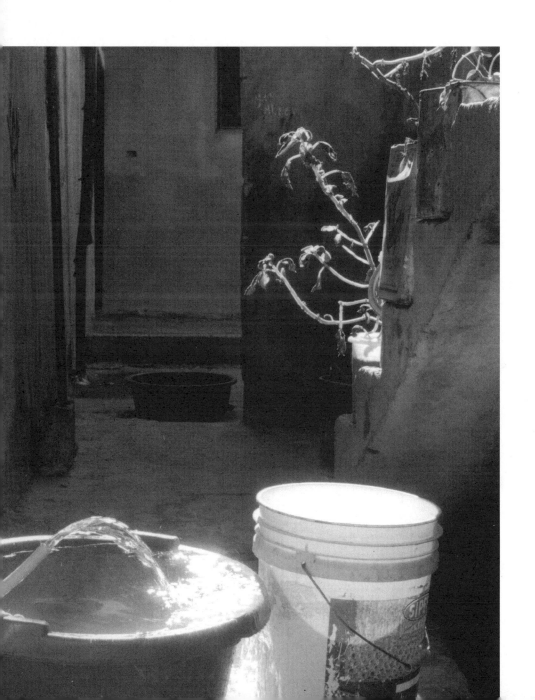

BEIRUT'S SUBURBAN FRINGE CHANGES ITS CHARACTER: A PLACE OF TOWERS IN THE PROTECTION OF POVERTY

Hasan Daoud

To reach the supermarket on the city's edge, we traversed some very narrow lanes, the first one branching off from the main boulevard. We found it in a massive building whose expanse seemed out of proportion with the alleys' restricted width.

On the level below the ground floor – but elevated from the garage – there was a space. Its exact use had not been settled on yet, and so it remained a garage. The young fellow, whose job it was to take the cars down below, told us to leave the key in the ignition. He drove the car down to the lower level, from which the dust rose to blanket the single exit/entrance. From the commotion, and then from the emptiness next to the sloping ramp, I realized that the crowding below was the same crowding caused by the density of automobiles in the narrow streets. But quite a few people were organizing the comings and goings to the garage, just as there were a large number of men standing at the entry of the supermarket. Throughout the city as well as in the outer neighbourhoods, advertisements up on billboards were proclaiming that this supermarket was open twenty-four hours a day.

Though it had not been receiving customers for long at all, the supermarket was already dilapidated from the constant throng of people, day and night. Even though it was packed with customers, the employees who restocked shelves with merchandise were hard at work, side by side with customers taking goods off the shelves to buy. The crowd spread throughout the two massive halls, blocking what was meant to be an opening between them, and also milling about in the space supposedly reserved for the electric room and toilets. Every possible space had been taken up by merchandise-laden shelves. The goods were stored outside this building, in a nearby structure, which might not have been finished. The billboard advertisements had also claimed that the prices here were lower than anywhere else. Rather than one reduction customers were allowed two, but the terms of the second one were so confusing that to understand it the customer had to hear an explanation directly from the supermarket employees. Some of the goods were indeed much cheaper than they would be elsewhere, and a few were offered for what amounted to a give-away, as reward for the customer who spent more than a certain sum of money. At six o'clock, when we were there, a shiver of anxiety ran through the crowd about whether there were enough of these items to go around. In the aisles between the shelves there was a great deal of move-ment: people seemed wary. They were competing over brand items even though they knew the shelf would be immediately replenished. There was a crowd at the four registers, and they were in a hurry as well.

The experiment in wooing customers away from the small shops in favour of the supermarket in the suburban area succeeded. And here on the suburban fringe, the contagion was not slow to spread. In fact, it moved so swiftly that one establishment was soon followed by another. On the broad main street, before we turned into the narrow lane, we saw another huge supermarket, the construction completed but the place not yet open. And on another road, after our visit, we spotted still another supermarket, also newly built. It looked as if the whole area had begun to exchange its identity.

This was not the first time. Throughout the past decade, the look of the outer neighbourhoods had been changed in stages. No longer were the homes here shacks – according to the worldwide definition or in the Third World sense – of metal sheeting, and no longer did they constitute a poverty belt encompassing the city. In the space of those ten or fifteen years, the area expanded ceaselessly, swelling with people; but its physical units had swollen as well. It was as

if, for instance, the tiny bread bakeries had become – in their enormity – bread factories. And the dry-goods shops, which were also located in basement or garage spaces, were larger and more grandiose than any in the city. The buildings rose higher and higher, and grew bigger and bigger, until on the main streets they came to be called 'centres' and 'towers'.

Here, on the city's new outskirts, development unvaryingly tends toward the immense, not only because of an increased level of consumption resulting from the density of population, but also because enormity has become a characteristic that distinguishes the suburb from the city. In the supermarket, the shelves do not bring together many varieties of goods, but the ones that are there require big lorries to transport them. Similarly, because the factories (and these suburban areas) do not use imported raw materials, they buy large quanitites of goods. If the suburban belt's merchants are vying with others with their low prices, it is because price reduction follows from large volume and, in turn, is the principle behind it.

As the suburban belt has consumed more landmass, new buildings have gone up on the ruins of houses, and food warehouses have replaced the shops. Instead of the suburbs being a nightly refuge for those who work by day in the city, people both work and live here now.

The factories, banks, markets, and commercial exchange firms have all moved into the area. Everything has been set up in the tiny lanes and interior streets, and also along the old streets that were laid out before the suburb even existed. Not a single major street has been added, nor has any existing street been widened. But that's sufficient, because the kernel of the suburban ring and its strength are not in the broad thoroughfares that encircle it but rather in the tiny arteries in the interior. That is, in the parts of it which remain invisible to those who live in the city proper.

To force the state to rebuild and make streets accessible once again, the commercial market that has gobbled up the entirety of one of these streets articulated its demand by invoking a solidarity and collective spirit about the suburb as an entity. The 'Association of Merchants of the Suburban Region' and the 'Manufacturing Association of the Suburban Region' are names that will resound in people's ears. The suburb is no longer to be defined as a belt of misery, or houses of tin, or a depressingly large tail that drags down the body of the city. Rather, it has become an entity complete in itself, having broken free of the body on which it grew. It has its own existence now, one equivalent to the city's and directly facing it. It is a single and unified entity counterpoised to the dispersed and divided that is the city, or the society that lacks solidarity. It is a unit of strength and poverty combined – or rather, a thing of strength that uses poverty as a means and is fortified by it. The markets, the towers, the factories, are not outside of the poverty, distanced from it, but are the institutions built upon poverty as a basic principle: they are poverty's supporting structures. This assumption of poverty as fundamental and permanent is evident in the developing wealth of some who ascribe to this belief and have added the elements which strengthen it.

The suburban space is another city, or an equivalent social space, one no longer content to simply stiffen its spine and suffer. For now it endeavours to gather all its parts together, and protect the rights of its subjects, there on the edges of the city.

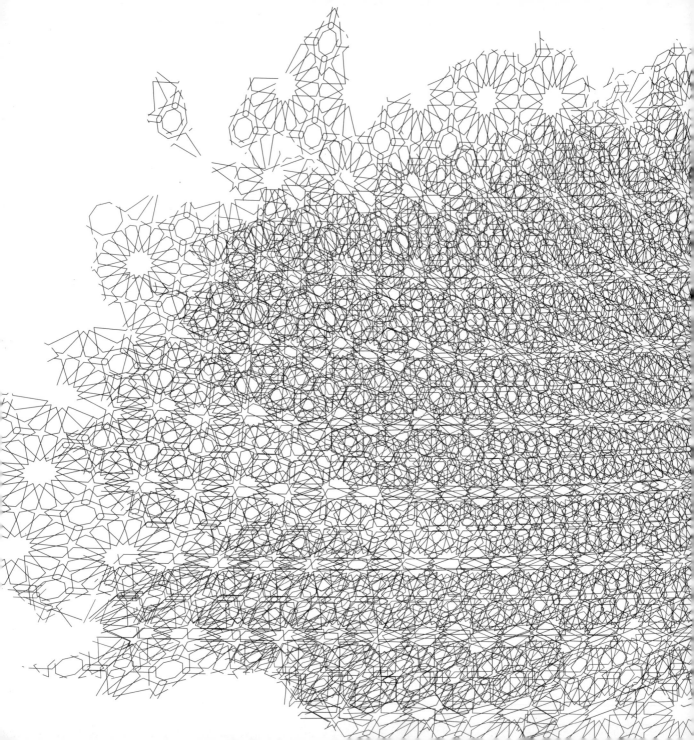

RESTLESS

SLUGGISH COUNTDOWN TO WAR

Abbas El-Zein

Photos by Dalia Khamissy

It has been raining all week, a persistent drizzle unlike the brief downpours that are more typical of Beirut. The city is slumbering. I am staying with my parents. My father goes out less often. My mother is snuggled under the blankets. She hopes the war won't happen. My niece is playing hopscotch softly. The kettle is boiling like a purring cat. The house is quiet. Rain is the soporific of cities.

A man strapped with dynamite walks into the HSBC bank in Hamra Street. Terrified staff hand over the money without delay. The robber then declares that he has stormed the bank to protest the impending invasion of Iraq. The bank is widely known as the British Bank. The minister of interior arrives on the scene and negotiates. A few minutes later, the robber releases his hostages in return for a press conference. The minister of interior takes the opportunity to explain to journalists the robber's motivations. The robber is later found to be deranged. Anti-colonialism has gone berserk. Conspiracy theorists claim that the robbery has been staged to make the minister of interior look good.

Alexander Downer beams on television for five memorable seconds. There is every chance, says Downer, that the war will start on Thursday. My brother-in-law asks me how come our 'plump minister of exterior' knows. I say Australia is part of the Coalition. He asks me how many soldiers Australia is contributing. I say two thousand. He bursts out laughing. He thinks it's a joke.

A friend of mine says he has come up with the ideal scenario for the war: the Americans swiftly invade; the Iraqis resist so hard that the Americans are soundly defeated; George W. Bush loses the next election; the Iraqi regime, weakened by the American assault, collapses, to be swiftly replaced by a pluralistic system of government modelled on Sweden. I compliment my friend on his vision. But why all this swiftness, I ask. 'To minimize civilian casualties,' he says. I shake my head.

The Turks have killed more Kurds than Saddam Hussein has ever dreamed of. The Israelis have enough nuclear bombs to kill all the Arabs and Jews of the Middle East. Saddam has a drone airplane incapable of dropping propaganda leaflets on the Kurds. The Americans will liberate the Iraqis whether they like it or not. The Iraqis will wish someone other than the Americans would do the job. I lecture my students on globalization, time-space compression and increased interconnectedness. I get back stares of detachment.

The rain has stopped. A soft winter sun shines over the Mediterranean. Snow covers the hills around Beirut. My father is at his office. My niece is walking barefoot around the house. The kettle is boiling again. My mother is about to go out. She asks me if war will break out after all. I say, undoubtedly. She has the feeling it won't.

The city is overrun with rumours about devil worshippers. They are said to kidnap children, kill them and drink their blood. They listen to certain kinds of music — heavy metal and black metal. They dig up corpses and arrange orgies. They take drugs and push each other to suicide. Like your average married couple, I point out to my worried sister. They come, we are told, from all geographical areas and sectarian backgrounds; they cannot be used as an excuse for starting a civil war. Parents anxiously watch their children. Tattoos are viewed with suspicion. Minor television clerics reveal that devil worshippers are good at hiding their real identities. They are not the same on the inside as the outside. Unlike George W. Bush and Alexander Downer. A mother reports her daughter to the police because she found a letter containing references to devil worshipping in the teenager's drawer. The girl claims the letter is a trap she set for her cousin whom she suspects of being a devil worshipper herself. And so it goes. Conspiracy theorists have never had it this good. Lebanese social neuroses are at work. East meets west in Lebanon every day, and the middle classes spend much energy consuming western products while weeding out undesired aspects of western culture, from open homosexuality and premarital sex to drugs and rap music, all of which is described as un-Lebanese behaviour. Not unlike the un-Australianness of some Australian crimes — shooting and gang rape are branded Lebanese, prostitution and counterfeiting are Russian while drug dealing is multiracial. The minister of interior in Lebanon goes on television to reassure the Lebanese that the rumours are false and that parents should watch out.

Australia's minister of exterior performs the same logical acrobatics that his British counterpart has shown himself capable of a few days earlier. Hence, the French threat of vetoing war made war more likely, and the Iraqis did not prove that they had no weapons of mass destruction. I have always been told that using two negatives in a sentence is to be avoided. It takes a war to make me understand how serious the problem is. Does the Australian Exterior include the British Interior or are Australians really British on the inside, albeit with a built-in delay? Up to seventy individuals suspected of devil worshipping have been investigated throughout Lebanon, but only a dozen have been detained. The general prosecutor says he cannot charge someone just because he wears ugly tattoos on his shoulders. And why not, says our neighbour. Alexander Downer has a strange look on his face. My parents' maid thinks twice before going out. I tell her Beirut is one of the safest cities I have ever been to. She giggles and probably thinks I am fool.

A poet publishes an article in a major daily addressed to God himself. If God is as good as He claims, how come He has created George W. Bush? Religious and political leaders in the conservative city of Tripoli are outraged. God should not be addressed in those terms, they insist. The next day the newspaper is banned from Tripoli.

I go to university. Given the latest turn in fashion, lecturers can now tell the colour of the underpants of many of their students. Other students wear headscarves, and I cannot tell the colour of their hair. Demonstrations and sit-ins every day. Sydney and

Melbourne march against the war. Some classes are suspended. My parents' maid is still worried. I check the rates of sexual crimes on the Interpol website. In 2000, you were nine times more likely to be sexually assaulted in Australia than in Lebanon.

War has started. Lebanon is dealing with a new deluge and its aftermath. It has rained non-stop for days. Landslides and drowned villages. Emergency procedures are activated. The army is called out. Severed heads and amputated limbs on Al Jazeera. The Arab street is boiling. My mother asks me to turn off the kettle. Thank God for Al Jazeera. My father is channel-hopping. Two thousand kangaroos are killed in Australia every year, says the Discovery channel. Alexander Downer leaps from CNN to the BBC in five seconds. Iraqi information minister Al-Sahhaf is sparring with Donald Rumsfeld. Will the Iraqis fight in Baghdad or won't they? My mother calls my sister to find out how long the war will last and whether parsley can be used with curry. The Americans complain about Al Jazeera. They see the expression of anti-western sentiment as anti-democratic. Thank God for Al Jazeera. Does it outweigh George W. Bush? We'll find out on judgment day. But will God be judged, and by whom? If things keep going this way, perhaps by Bush. I won't be going to Tripoli soon.

A bomb explodes at a McDonald's restaurant in Dawra on the main road to Tripoli. Small bombs have been going off occasionally at American-brand food outlets at night, leaving no casualties. This one is different.

A Bali-style set-up, with one bomb inside and one outside, and the two are not the same. A few grams of explosives in the toilet to be followed by fifty kilograms of TNT in the car park. But the delay mechanism of the big one did not function. Alexander Downer fails to repeat Jack Straw's speech from three days ago.

Edward Said speaks to a packed amphitheatre at the university. He has grown a beard and looks like a tired Che Guevara. He is as eloquent as ever, despite his leukaemia. He wants us to save Humanism from the onslaught of Structuralism and Post-Structuralism. On which side is Donald Rumsfeld, I wonder. Al-Sahhaf is still fighting. Conspiracy theorists are interviewed by Al Jazeera. Osama bin Laden's recruitment officers are said to be having a field day, with more converts than Iraqi POWs. History is in the making – a guaranteed supply of corpses for the next fifty years.

I take a stroll in the beautifully restored old city of Beirut. Dark thoughts keep me company. Will all this be destroyed again? War does not seem to have affected the Lebanese economy. The underclass – foreign workers from Sri Lanka, Ethiopia and Syria – is as over-exploited as ever. The old construction sites are still abandoned by their bankrupt owners. Valet parking is thriving, still absorbing a good portion of the workforce. Child beggars are active at major road junctions and entertainment centres. The trendy restaurants of Monot are packed. The night-clubs are preparing for the evening. The streets are full of potential devil worshippers. I walk home after sunset. I savour the hushed liveliness of the backstreets, emanating from the charming seven- and eight-storey buildings. This is the Arab street that I know and love – in Beirut, Damascus and Baghdad – and there is nothing revolutionary about it. I get home. Al Jazeera says the Arab world is changing. My niece has strained her left ankle. My mother thinks the war is a lie. I am reading Baudrillard. My father wants his tea. Some things will never change.

Baghdad falls like the long-dead leaf of an autumn tree. It's spring in Beirut. I am back in Sydney to a mild Australian winter. Leichhardt cannot decide if it's Italian or English. A colleague at work asks me how my trip went and inquires about the situation in Saudi Arabia. A friend of mine is just back from Portugal. I quiz her about the situation in Belgium. She stares at me, uncomprehending. Alexander Downer is making sense. New billboards have come up on the way to university, advertising an anti-suicide association. 'Want to end it all,' the logo says, referring to suicide itself. The logo would equally work for a suicide-assistance service. The national museum is looted a few hours after Baghdad falls. Everyone blames the Americans. The Pentagon is supposed to be fighting to take over Baghdad while protecting its buildings from looters. No wonder Americans are so arrogant: even their critics expect them to behave like Gods.

Iraqi army officers demonstrate against the presence of US soldiers at the Iraqi Ministry of Defence. The national library is burned down, a week after Baghdad is secured. What excuse can I come up with for the US this time? The Americans distribute a list of wanted members of the Iraqi regime on a deck of cards. American soldiers must be entertained at all times. Is this the playfulness of the new empire? Al-Sahhaf, the only Iraqi to have tried to keep the Americans out of Baghdad, is trying to surrender. 'We're not interested,' say the Americans over a game of poker. The devil smiles devilishly. Al-Sahhaf is offered a job by an Arab satellite television based in Riyadh. 'If only we could find him,' the station manager says.

I am back in Beirut. Scantily-clad women stare at me reproachfully from billboard posters next to the HSBC bank in Hamra. Are you coming yet, they seem to be saying. Why am I being titillated, out in the open, on a major road? I thought advertising is about selling products. I can hardly buy the lingerie or sanitary pads these women are promoting. I avert my eyes and concentrate on my driving. I tell my students about global consciousness, advertising, the invasiveness of financial capital and the recession of public space. I say nothing about the private interests trying to reach my crotch. I wax philosophical about the changing nature of the nation state. The students in the front row are glassy-eyed. Are they sleeping or cogitating? A US company is awarded the reconstruction of the port of Basra. The American envoy to Iraq says America is not interested in governing Iraq. I believe him. The colonizer wants access to resources but not governance. Neo-colonialism is born.

My mother goes to the memorial of a relative killed twenty-one years ago by Saddam Hussein. Clothes and a skeleton have been found in one of the mass graves. A suicide-assistance NGO, Dignitas, is investigated by the Swiss authorities. The Arab world is staying the same. Australia passes a law declaring Hizbullah a terrorist organization. A new government is formed in Lebanon. The minister of interior is still the same, on the inside and the outside. Syria has tightened its control on Lebanon, ahead of a possible confrontation with the US. Lebanon is a client state of Syria. Australia is a client state of the US. Syria is flirting with the US. The US is bullying Syria. Australia is slipping into shabby colonial clothes.

An attractive woman, in black and white, advertises Gitanes cigarettes on billboard posters in Mkalles. Her lips are painted in striking dark blue. *Liberte toujours*, the logo says. Are blue lips attractive or is this a kiss of death? Tobacco advertising must have been infiltrated by anti-smoking campaigners or pro-suicide activists. The devil is having a field day. Advertisers are devoid of irony. Syria has banned tobacco advertising twenty years ago. Smoking is reaching epidemic levels in Syria. Lebanese satellite television stations beam tobacco ads all day to the Arab world. The Syrian army controls Lebanon. Lebanese advertising is cancer to Syrians. Lebanese shrewdness is no match for Syrian intelligence.

Bombs go off in Riyadh and Casablanca. My colleague at work asks me about the situation in Iran. The Moroccans are fighting terrorism. They introduce the death penalty for a wide range of offences. 'Now you can be hanged for wearing the burnoose the wrong way,' I tease our Moroccan visitor. So what, says our neighbour. In which Kuwaiti hotel are Australian soldiers staying, asks my brother-in-law. Alexander Downer is on his way to Iraq. The Iraqis are worried about their future. At least the war is over. War? What war, says my mother. Australia will help reorganize the Iraqi Ministry of Agriculture. Wheat is the biggest Australian export to Iraq. I tell my students about the floating capital — deregulated, on a rampage, a gun in one hand, a spreadsheet in another. My students are deeply worried. They want to know about their assignments.

My niece is no longer limping. Her feet have grown a size bigger. The Arab world is changing. My father's tea is a shade darker. My mother doesn't care. Summertime is upon us. The jacaranda trees are blossoming. There is a yellow flower carpet in front of our building. Saddam Hussein's face is crossed out on the walls of Baghdad. The devil is omniscient. George W. Bush smiles at me. God is nowhere to be seen. The world slips by, like sand through my fingers.

HEY
HANDSOME

Nabeel Kaakoush

● Excuse me, *monsieur*, do you have the time? · ● Sure, it's 1.30 AM.

● Uh-huh. Hey, got a cigarette?
● Yeah, help yourself.

● What are you doing here? · ● Waiting ...

● For whom?
● Someone. And you?

● Just cruising around, killing time … where you from?

● From around here … where you from? · ● Also. What do you do?

والله هلق ماشي

ليه ؟

●Gosh, right now, nothing! · ●Why?

كنت عم بشتغل بمحل وسكروا

ليه ما بتدور
ع شي تاني ؟!

●Used to work in a shop that closed down. · ●So why don't you look for something else?

- Man, they're all after university degrees.
- Yeah, you're right.

- Life is shitty … My mom is sick and I have to buy her medicine … and my sister's still in school.

- And your dad, where's he?
- Fuck him! Nobody knows where the hell he is!

- Sorry … OK, let me help you …
- How?

- We'll figure it out … You come here often?
- From time to time … Depends …

- Depends on what? … Fine, get in, let's go for a drive.

● Where to? · ● Wherever you like. Where would you like to end up?

● Let's go up to the mountains. · ● Whatever. But it's a long drive and there's traffic … plus, it's gonna cost you …

اديه يعني؟

● How much, then?

بدك تكسب سونت دولار ...

اوف!
بسن كتير هيك

انو ما تنسى بدنا نعيش
وكمان عندي احار البيت ...
بعدين ما بتحرز

● About $100. · ●Whoa, that's a lot · ●Don't forget, I've got to survive and I also have the rent to think about ... otherwise, it ain't worth it.

طيب . بعطيك . ١٠٠
ع يومين . بين
عليك Desperate

يالله ... كلو منيح ... مشي

● Fine … I'll give you $100 for two nights … You seem kinda desperate.
● Cool … it's all good … let's go.

Translated from Arabic by Sarah al-Hamad
©Nabeel Kaakoush 2003

BEIRUT'S ATHLETES CELEBRATE THE DEFEAT OF CHOLESTEROL WITH FLOWERS AND CHOCOLATE

Hasan Daoud

Photos by Dalia Khamissy

People exercising on the Corniche in Beirut number in the thousands these days. They head for the city's seaside promenade as early as four AM, and the stream of enthusiasts continues to flow until about nine. Six o'clock (in the morning, of course) is the absolute high point. At that time the area is packed with people walking, running or standing near the metal balustrade, practising Swedish exercises. Or they're below, swimming in the sea, and are as likely to be in the water on clear winter mornings as they are during the days of summer. Or they're congregating in the broad open area near the Hotel Qadmus to perform group exercises led by a fellow named Nizar Sultani.

In the space facing the hotel, they exercise every day beginning precisely at six in the morning. Those who are five or ten minutes late, join when they arrive. There are exercises to harden the scapula, for example, or perhaps to strengthen their calves. Yet, even though they show up steadfastly every day, they do not know (as the real athletes do) the names for all of the movements. Instead they speculate which muscles they think are benefiting from each exercise. This is due to the fact that they are not true, authentic athletes. They came to athletic pursuits late, at the age of forty for instance, or fifty. That is why they know how much progress they've made not by a muscle's thickness and increasing firmness, but rather from the amount of fat they've lost around their bellies and waists (in particular). Their knowledge comes also from lengthy print-outs which they obtain from specialists. There is much attention given to cholesterol and triglycerides.

They're forty, fifty, perhaps they have even reached the age of eighty or ninety. The Sheikh of Runners – his absence was lamented by the president of the Republic in his address on the occasion of Independence Day and Science Day – is between eighty and ninety years of age. At the start of his nineties he wrote on his athletic shirt his name and title, and specified his age at the time as 'over eighty'. Not only does the Sheikh of Runners run on the Corniche, but he often leaves his mates behind here and goes off to represent them in America or Europe where, despite his age, he runs nothing short of forty-five kilometres.

And if that isn't enough, he is also a propagandist when it comes to sports. During the past two years he worked tirelessly to bring together the exercise buffs in some sort of club or association. He went about asking them for personal photos to place on membership cards he planned to distribute to them. Actually, the association never got off the ground. After all, the folks who go down to the Corniche do not really want to be athletes or to be identified as such. It's only an hour they spend there, on the Corniche, after which they return to their occupations. They can be counted in the thousands, yet no sort of collective identity has taken shape and no association has been formed. For example, they only say good morning to the people they know. And by about nine they all leave the Corniche, together, abandoning it to the strolling families who occupy it in the evening. The Corniche isn't theirs – the athletes – and they are not its particular group or party, to the point where – in the spacious open area where they perform their exercises together – they've

begun almost to sense that the Hotel Qadmus, which was recently refurbished and reopened, will in the very near future insist they find another place to exercise.

The shared presence of these people in their thousands has not yielded any new organisation, and there is no group sentiment that brings them together. Even the firms who produce soda and chocolate, and the sportswear agencies that fill the city with their advertisements, haven't erected a single billboard along the Corniche. Even though they all wear running shoes and training suits, the companies and agencies do not take them seriously, or perhaps they are not aware of their existence. Or, perhaps they are aware but know that these exercise buffs, despite their numbers, are not the people who create and shape public opinion.

Yesterday, about a hundred people gathered in that same open space where they do their group exercises. It was six o'clock, the time for their exercise programme, but instead of immersing themselves in the movements that enhance their bodies they began to hand out flowers to each other. Just like that, as if they were celebrating the birthday of someone in the group. Then, they distributed pieces of chocolate which perhaps, on any other day, they would avoid eating because of the high caloric content. But they were in the midst

of a celebration. When it was time for a little speech by the Sheikh of Runners, what he said did not overjoy them: he really wanted, he declared, to see Beirut's entire population exercising on the Corniche. But for them, these exercise sessions embody a deeply held principle, and they don't want their daily attendance to signify that exercise has triumphed over all other pursuits. They are here, men and women, in order to celebrate their daily morning gathering. It seems to be a sort of birthday celebration for Nizar Sultani, who volunteers his time to train them every day, and who is transformed into their wonderful and gentle guru every morning for one hour. He urges them gently to perform the movements if he sees that they're just going through the motions and not really exercising. Perhaps he even scolds them, but in a nice way. It's a gala to honour Nizar Sultani, one of them told me. Every year, we salute him on a day such as this. When Nizar Sultani stood on the stone bench so that he could see the large crowd, he said a word of thanks, with an embarrassed smile. His words were the antithesis of the Sheikh of Runners's speech, read from a piece of paper in formal Arabic. The Sheikh likes to see all the exercise buffs as a single group – a victory for Exercise. And so, as the morning festivity came to a close, they watched while the Sheikh hung a medal on the chest of Nizar Sultani and awarded him a silver cup.

NO PLACE LIKE HOME

Leila M.

.AGE 10 — GOD

While playing chase in a friend's garden one sunny afternoon in south London, a statue fell on my six-year-old sister's head.

In the stark intensive care unit I found my mother bent over her hospital bed, crying and praying in Arabic. Her emotions and screams felt alien and theatrical echoing around the walls of St Mary's. 'Mummy please stop doing it like that,' I shouted. 'The God here won't understand you,' I continued with conviction. This brought on another wave of frenzy from my frantic mother who, I now believe, was crying over my sister's condition as much as over my confused wisdom. Thankfully my sister recovered consciousness the following week.

.AGE 11 — BOOT CAMP

I know I should be grateful for not having spent my formative years under a showering of bombs, but to the non-war experienced, the Arabic School was as close to boot camp as a nine-year-old could imagine. As an undetected dyslexic, I was struggling enough with mastering the English language without the pressure to learn a lingo that I hardly ever used. Predicting a lack of enthusiasm each week the sadistic teachers, with starched fringes poking out of their hijabs, would pace the corridors and guard the gates for any latecomers, or those like myself who lingered close to the exits, dreaming up ways to escape.

It seemed cruel justice to spend Saturday afternoons at an Arabic school on the other side of London, learning the *ayet el kursey* (one of the main Qur'anic prayers), when every other child was watching *Tizwas*. My brother and I were in our teens — him trying to look cool sporting a George Michael hairdo and wristbands, and myself in a hand-painted denim jacket screaming the word 'unique' on my back. As there were only three classes at the school, my fellow classmates were an assortment of refugee kids, middle-class kids and geeks, aged seven to ten. In a class of beginners, I was not only the weirdest, but also the oldest kid. It's hard to be cool and ooze attitude when you're competing with people whose ages are less than your shoe size — especially when they could read better then you.

In a bid to keep my dignity and avoid the humiliation of not knowing my *Alef-Ba-Ta,* I resorted to drastic measures. I painstakingly transcribed the Qur'anic text we were supposed to learn into a sort of coded phonetic English, in faint pencil. This was possible due to a Syrian neighbour who helped me transcribe the homework each day after school. It was excruciating work. The pencil markings had to be faint so my parents wouldn't spot them, but I had to be able to read them. It all seemed worth it at the time. I became skilled in the art of deception like a well-trained actress, and even allowed for the occasional dramatic pause to show how hard I had studied.

All was going well, until one afternoon a substitute teacher, with a particularly evil streak, caught me when he noticed my eyes were reading my book from left to right. Snatching it from my hand he looked in utter disgust at my English pencil markings and informed the class that what I had done was blasphemous and God would punish me. Just to make sure I was under no illusion that I was going to meet my maker and deal with my punishment at a later date, he took it upon himself to unleash the wrath of the Almighty on the spot before the class with the aid of an old wooden ruler.

I ran away at lunchtime.

.AGE 12 – DOGS AND THE LEBANON

One of my best friends at school was Cynthia Stewart. One Easter, I had the pleasure of accompanying the Stewart family to their rural retreat that they shared with Granny Lilly and her unmarried daughter Rachelle, aka Aunt Hitler, and her loud excitable dog Bingo. I say Aunt Hitler because she was fierce and wore a kind of house uniform and a tight hair bun that reminded Cynthia and I of German pictures we saw in our history classes.

I spent much of the holiday avoiding Aunt Hitler and hiding from Bingo. I had an inexplicable phobia of dogs. I believed that they were dumb and violent, and no one in my house seemed to disagree. So despite the fact that Bingo was a tiny sausage dog that couldn't do anything but yelp, I was crippled when he was anywhere near me. For Aunt Hitler, the uneasy relationship I had with the animal kingdom was very understandable when she explained to us all over a Sunday roast after Cynthia asked me how I could possibly be afraid of such a tiny thing. 'Well, it's easy to answer that,' Aunt Hitler interrupted in a thoroughly self-assured tone. 'It's because they eat dogs in the Lebanon, of course,' she said while staring me straight in the eye. 'What, like hot dogs?' Cynthia responded with a contagious laughter that put everyone, excluding Aunt Hitler, in hysterics.

A few hours later, it didn't seem so funny and I spent the journey home wondering if it could be true.

.AGE 15 — THE DINNER PARTIES

Despite my attempt to avoid Arabs, there was no getting away from them, especially at the monthly dinner party my parents threw. It was a kind of cultural monthly Anglo-Arab *soirée*.

There were Shi'ites, Sunnis, Christians, atheists, pacifists and just about anyone who had an interest in Arab issues, including British and French journalists, artists, authors, broadcasters and poets. Everyone had an opinion about the state of the Middle East and was keen to share it. Each dinner was a frantic affair that would challenge the most efficient event organizer. I could never work out how my parents managed to invite everyone without sending invitations, or how my mother could handle such complex catering for the forty-plus dinner guests, mostly on her own, with a little help from friends. I used to hate those parties. We had a rule in my house that I could be as scruffy as I liked with my friends, but had to wear what my parents told me to when they entertained. It seemed like a good compromise until those dreaded party weekends when I would be forced to don frilly white shirts, velvet skirts and plaid tights. My brother and I were on entertainment duty. We had to look after all of the children who accompanied the adults, around eight to ten kids, including our two younger sisters. For the most part, everyone entertained themselves, thanks to a well-stocked archive of videos like *My Little Pony,* and Marvel comics.

Most of the adults would get drunk while telling stories or singing songs. There was always an *oud,* usually a microphone and most defiantly a sing-along. Much of the music was of Um Kulthum or Fayruz, although I couldn't have told you that at the time, for to my ears it was revolting noise pollution. I used to eagerly wait for the neighbours downstairs to come up and complain so that the tipsy guests would be forced to leave and the racket would stop. But most of the time my parents would invite them in, and any complaints would be forgotten over a glass of whisky.

.AGE 16 – THE KISS

Having my mother spit in my face after school one day was not the response I expected from asking if she had a good day.

I met him at a crap party. I was there to help a friend who needed an alibi to see her boyfriend because of her strict father. I didn't have many Arab friends, and although he was not someone I would have normally spoken to, he was polite and sat long enough for my girlfriend to decide whether she was still girlfriend and boyfriend. We made small talk. He tried to teach me a few Arabic words. Then, he asked for my number, and offered to walk me to the tube station.

So we walked and talked. Well, he talked, and I responded. Don't recall much about his conversation except that he asked a lot of questions and had a thick Arabic accent and smelled of cheap aftershave. While walking at a steady pace, he grabbed my arm with one hand and my head with the other, and tried to kiss me. It was an unexpected and unwelcome move that left me screaming at him in my limited Arabic. Ashamed and angry, he made a swift exit and that was the end of that as far as I was concerned. Except, it wasn't. The following day while I was at school, his mother called my mother and asked if she knew that I had been kissing boys. His mother also informed my mother that I had offered to sleep with her precious son, but because he was a good boy he had refused and walked me to the station instead to make sure I didn't get into trouble. Hence, my mother's unreasonable reactionary face-spitting. She was not upset by the fact that it might be true because she knew it was a classic case of shit-stirring. She was frustrated that even the simplest situations were distorted by interfering Arabs who should know better. Despite the physical distance between London and Beirut, there was no escaping it.

.AGE 21 - THE GRADUATION, THE DEADLINE AND THE INEVITABLE DECISION TO TRY

They all met. They all frowned. He didn't understand them. They didn't like him. His socks were disgusting or so my mother's friends informed me. He was a college beau and they were my family. They had come to attend my graduation. He didn't stand a chance really. And despite our combined efforts, they just didn't want to know. What concerned them more was the idea that I had lived in a rough student flat with several girls and the place was falling apart. 'Don't go up if you don't want your heart to hurt,' said my mother in soap opera fashion as she passed another concerned parent conducting their own inspection. My flatmates and I had feverishly spent the day preparing for their arrival, hiding evidence of the opposite sex and too many takeaways. We hid the stuff of late nights in the washing machine, under the stairs, inside the boiler and frozen, hot water pipes.

I was given funding and a three-month deadline to find a media job before being shipped out to Beirut to join the rest of the family. I didn't want to go. I was in love with my parentless London and convinced I would find a way to stay. But as the summer wound down and college friends started buying suits, I knew it was inevitable and I cried all the way to the airport.

.THE MOVE

'How is it that, one day life is orderly and you are content. A little cynical perhaps, but on the whole just so, and then, without warning, you find the solid floor is a trap door and you are now in another place whose geography is uncertain and whose customs are strange.'

I read and recited that passage from Jeanette Winterson's book *The Passion* daily like a mantra. It summed up the hysterical situation I found myself living in post-war Beirut. There was, in my initial and very English opinion, very little reason to stay there. I walked into a world of tired people and broken buildings, and was ill equipped for the intricate social customs and religious divisions that I encountered daily. The war was officially over, yet a dollar war was raging just as fiercely and despite the silence of the sectarian conflict, there was still an unmissable divide. Each side had their own media, own clubs, and even their own airport. In a country half the size of Wales, you didn't have to be well versed in the ins and outs of Lebanon's history to know something wasn't quite right. My father had raised me to take the best of two cultures and avoid anything extreme; yet, moving to Beirut, there seemed to be nothing but extremes. If people partied, they did it with abandon and without thought of tomorrow. If they drank, they got exceedingly pissed, and if they ate out, they had to order enough for the entire neighbourhood. The electricity supply was scarce, yet you seldom saw an ungroomed lady on the streets.

The initial plan had been to spend a few months, meet the family, get a tan and get the hell out of there. It was an awkward introduction after three hedonistic years as a student. Yet despite all this, I didn't fit in. I was utterly seduced by the craziness of the city and within months I began to live the good life. My pigeon Arabic evolved under the watchful eye of new-found friends and as the weeks turned into months, thoughts of my other reality in London were but a distant memory until a friend from there called to ask if I had been kidnapped. 'Please phone me from the British Embassy so I know you're not being held against your will. If you don't call by tomorrow morning I will contact them and ask them to go and find you,' my well-meaning friend said in a serious tone.

I spent several years in Beirut, growing, laughing and surrounded by the love of friends and family. I also learned to love myself. How such a reluctant visitor could reap such love was a wonder until ...

.THE 7-YEAR ITCH

Imagine a life where every moment felt like *déjà vu* – what you said, where you went and what you did. Where every day was Sunday. Being partial to a bit of variety, and someone, who always loved the flavour of Wednesdays and Thursdays, it was time to jump ship and swim to another shore.

.THE RETURN

I was only away for seven years, and took frequent visits back to London throughout. Yet moving back to London was a surprise. Well, actually it was a slap in the face, a stinging, sharp slap that leaves a mark on your cheek, one that still feels warm at the first sign of trouble.

.THERE'S NO PLACE LIKE HOME

Whenever I need a dose of national pride, I take the bus and go to Edgware Road. It reminds me of all that is good, bad, ugly and great about the culture some of us can proudly call our own. Whenever I miss all that is home, I call my Teta and eat a *shawarma* sandwich. The need to find home is no longer desperate, and judging by the range of scrappy apartments I have rented over the past few years, that may not be such a bad thing. I'm not suggesting that home is a place where you can get a *shawarma* sandwich with *toum* (garlic), but maybe, just maybe, home is a place you can pick up a phone, or perhaps … home is a place inside your head where you can take the good bits of two cultures and fuse them to become a member of your own cultural party. For now, home could be Hamra Street in a sound clash with Hoxton Square, and sometimes, home is swimming in Jiyeh and coming out of the water at Brighton pier and speaking Cantonese or Welsh. I almost dread finding it because I'm worried that I won't like it, or that I shall love it so much that I'll never leave, and besides, the 'God' there might not speak English.

CONTRIBUTORS

HASAN DAOUD is chief editor of 'Nawafez' (Windows), the cultural supplement for *Al-Mustaqbal Daily* in Beirut. He has also served as cultural editor and contributor to other Lebanese national newspapers. His novels include *House of Mathilde* (in English by Granta, 1999, and in French by Actes Sud, 2000), *The Penguin's Song* (1998) and *Added Days* (1990, both Lenos Publishing House). He has also translated English novels into Arabic.

ANTOINE BOULAD, poet and director of the International College in Beirut, is a founding member of the Assabil Foundation, which aims to establish local libraries throughout Lebanon.

RACHID EL DAIF is the author of eleven works of fiction and poetry. He is best known internationally for his novel *Dear Mr Kawabata* (1999), which has been translated into eight languages. El Daif lives in Beirut and teaches Arabic language and literature at the Lebanese University.

ZEINA B. GHANDOUR practised law and worked in peace-keeping and post-conflict reconstruction in Asia, Africa, the Caribbean, Balkans and Middle East for the UN, EU and OSCE (the Organisation for Security and Co-operation in Europe), and as an elections monitor consultant for the British Foreign Office. Her first novel was *Honey* (Quartet Books, 1999). Currently she is at the London School of Economics, studying for a doctorate on the impact of the British Mandate on the customary law of Palestine.

ZIAD HALWANI is currently employed as an assistant manager in charge of music production projects at La CDThèque, in Achrafiye, Beirut. He has also worked as a freelance cook and food stylist for movies and books.

NABIL ISMAIL has been a photojournalist in Lebanon, since 1980. He worked as head of the photo department for AFP (Agence France-Presse) in Lebanon and Syria, from 1984 to 1995, and for the International Picture Agency in Beirut, from 1995 to 1999. Former president of the Lebanese Photojournalists' Syndicate, he is presently the head of the photo department for *Al-Mustaqbal Daily*.

NABEEL KAAKOUSH graduated in June 2003 with a bachelor's degree in graphic design from the Lebanese American University (LAU) in Beirut, where he is presently studying for a master's degree in business. He has taken part in Beirut design exhibitions, and won the Red Cross ICRC 'Women Facing War' poster competition in 2003. His fanzine *Ya Helo* (Hey Handsome) was part of his final project in graphic design at LAU where his research was about sexually abused children and prostitution.

KAMAL KASSAR, a lawyer by profession, studied classical flute at the Conservatoire National de Musique in Beirut and is a founding member of the music association *Résonnance*. He composed the music for Jalal Khoury's plays *Rafiq Sejaan* (1974) and *Hindiya* (1999). Kassar also wrote the script for Maroun Baghdadi's film *Little Wars* (1982) and filmed his own documentary on tobacco workers in south Lebanon.

MAHER KASSAR grew up in Lebanon and France, and holds an engineering degree from McGill University in Montreal. He is a genuine lover of cooking and food in all its forms. His passion has helped him rediscover the people, places and tastes of his country of origin.

DALIA KHAMISSY, a freelance photojournalist, has been working for ZAWAYA, a cultural magazine for Arab youth, since 2002. Last March, she was the photographer for a humanitarian mission in Iraq, and her black and white photos were published in ZAWAYA, As-Safir, a Lebanese daily newspaper, and in MERIP (Middle East Research and Information Project), Washington DC. Since 2001, she has also been the photographer for the Bulletin for Students' Rights, published by the Movement for People's Rights, a Lebanese NGO.

LEILA M., an Anglo-Arabic cultural supernova, is a full-time media junkie and part-time Arab who currently lives in London. Her ongoing passions include Mecca Cola, promoting Arabic hip hop, and the word 'Yes'. 'No Place Like Home' is her first short story.

REINE MAHFOUZ has been working as a photographer since 1999. She has exhibited her work in Lebanon and Europe. Last year, her exhibition in Stuttgart, Germany, featured photographs of the Palestinian refugee camps in Lebanon.

LENA MERHEJ, who has a master's degree in fine arts in design and technology from Parsons School of Design in New York, has worked as an animator, art director, freelance designer and lecturer. In 2002, her animated film Drawing the War was shown in the Sixth Annual MadCat Women's International Film Festival, in San Francisco.

OMAR SABBAGH was educated at Exeter College, Oxford University. He spent part of a gap year in Beirut, studying Arabic and becoming better acquainted with the city where his parents lived until the beginning of the civil war. Currently studying for a master's degree in English literature at King's College at the University of London, he is a passionate bibliophile and collector, and is fascinated by the animal kingdom.

HAZIM SAGHIE is a Lebanese writer and journalist. After working for As-Safir newspaper in Beirut in the 1970s and 1980s, he is now editor of the political weekly supplement 'Tayyarat' (Currents) for Al-Hayat. He also co-edits Abwab (Doors), a cultural quarterly published in Arabic. Saghie has published several books in Arabic, including works on Umm Kulthum and the cultures of Khomeinism. In English, he has published The Predicament of the Individual in the Middle East (Saqi Books, 2000).

NADINE R.L. TOUMA, an artist and writer, was spurred by the high incidence of plastic surgery in Beirut – in her words, 'western noses on eastern faces' – and made 6,000 marzipan noses and sold them from a vegetable truck on the streets of Beirut. Her install-ation, 'Haremharassment: Cairo St Courtship', first shown in the 2003 exhibition *Harem Fantasies and the New Scheheraza*des in the Centre de Cultura Contemporania de Barcelona, is presently on tour in Europe. Her short film *Bint 3Ayleh* (She Comes from a Good Family) was featured in the 2003 International Exhibitionist art series, a short season of art films in London.

FADI TUFAYLI, a journalist since 1996, has worked for *Al-Nahar* and *As-Safir* newspapers in Beirut. He is currently a writer and editor for the cultural supplement 'Nawafez' (Windows) for *Al-Mustaqbal Daily*. A graduate of the Lebanese University of Beirut, where he studied interior architecture, a collection of his poetry, *Aw Akthar* (Or More), has been published (Dar Al Intishar Al Arabi, 2000).

ABBAS EL-ZEIN studied engineering at the American University of Beirut and the University of Southampton. His novel *Tell the Running Water*, set during the civil war, was published in Sydney by Hodder Headline (Sceptre, 2001). He has written essays on migration, war and identity for Australian literary magazines. He is currently lecturer of environmental health at the American University of Beirut.

EDITORS

MALU HALASA has been published by the *Guardian*, *Financial Times* and *Times*, in London. For four years, she was the features editor of *Tank* magazine. She is the managing editor of the Prince Claus Fund Library in the Netherlands.

ROSEANNE SAAD KHALAF is Assistant Professor of English and coordinator of Creative Writing at the American University of Beirut. Her publications include: *Once Upon a Time in Lebanon*, and *Lebanon: Four Journeys to the Past*. She was the co-editor of *Themes*, a twelfth-grade English textbook for the National Centre for Educational Research and Development, in Beirut. She is currently working on a memoir and a series of children's books.

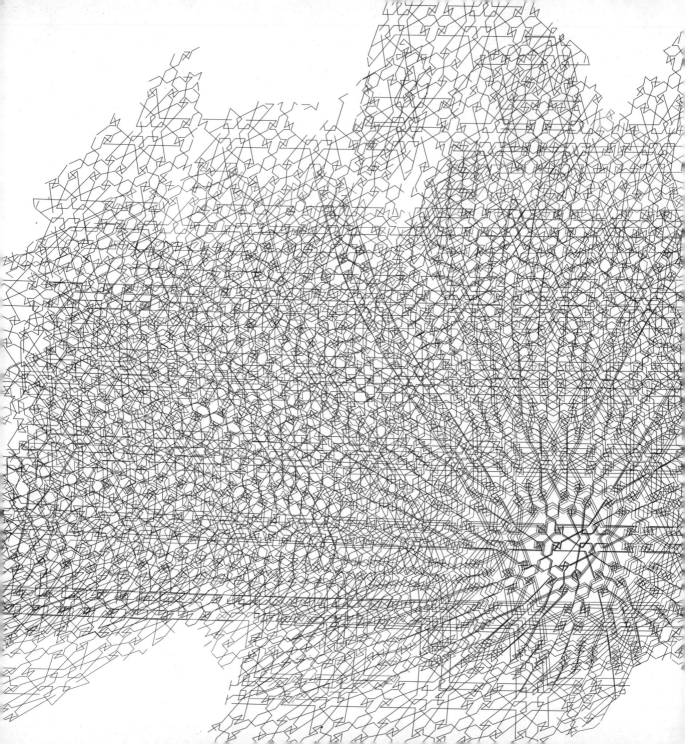